TIME IS
MONEY

TIME IS MONEY

A guide to selling
your Professional Services

By Richard F. Creedy

E. P. Dutton   New York

For information contact: Elsevier-Dutton Publishing Co., Inc., 2 Park Avenue, New York, N.Y. 10016

Library of Congress Cataloging in Publication Data

Creedy, Richard F
Time is money.
1. Self-employed. 2. Professions.
3. Business consultants. 4. Small business.
I. Title.
HD8036.C73 1980   658'.041   79-27216

ISBN: 0-525-93114-7

Published simultaneously in Canada by
Clarke, Irwin & Company Limited, Toronto and Vancouver

Designed by Mary Gale Moyes

10 9 8 7 6 5 4 3 2 1

First Edition

This book is dedicated to my wife, Pat, who has willingly shared our independent life-style and graciously given it the kind of enthusiasm, practicality, and encouragement that have made this book possible. The book is also dedicated to my daughter, Leslie, and my son, Jeffrey, who are a constant inspiration and strength.

CONTENTS

PREFACE

I have always wanted to work on my own. When I started nearly twenty years ago I found myself immediately surrounded by new puzzles.

My search for practical information and organized approaches was prompted by personally painful doubts and questions as well as experiences like these: My selling efforts did not produce sales. My pricing was founded more on rumor than logic. My casual attitude toward management and record keeping not only reduced efficiency but substantially increased taxes.

The organized approaches to these and other subjects suggested in this book have produced several specific results. Among them are: an enormous increase in personal confidence; the elimination or substantial reduction of doubt, confusion, anxiety, and wasted effort; a matching and satisfying increase in personal productivity; an increase in income of almost 300% in one year; a growing sense of control including a far more positive feeling about economic security in retirement.

Since taking the step of starting your own consulting or freelancing service may involve doing new things, the book is organized so that you can select subjects that interest you—get working information—and then do those things *your way* from a more confident base. The method suggested is simply to tackle one new thing at a time—do it until you feel comfortable—and steadily build believable and reliable levels of confidence that will help you get the results you want.

ACKNOWLEDGMENTS

I would like to first acknowledge the unflagging encouragement of Dr. Edward J. Mortola, president of Pace University, who over the years has been both a warm personal friend and loyal mentor.

In the course of collecting information over many years, I have read articles and books, listened to lectures, speeches, and presentations, and had many lively conversations with friends and associates to identify and explore relevant subjects. Appreciation is expressed here to these many sources some of which remain anonymous due to the passage of time.

In the course of actual preparation, I have conferred with many seasoned and experienced men and women in business and the professions. I particularly acknowledge and appreciate the guidance of two highly articulate and professional certified public accountants—Martin H. Bodian and C. Douglas Pettit. Their help has been critical in the preparation of the chapters "Price Your Service" and "Make Your Service Profitable."

Especially constructive guidance has come from the experience of many working professionals including bankers, lawyers, sales executives, top management executives, partners, professors, owners of services and others. I am particularly grateful to Henry Allen, Jay Bair, Arthur Bellaire, Lee Bloom, Ray Ellis, Justin Casey, Donald Chapin, Michael Civetta, Charles Colby, John Creedy, Judith Creedy, Stephen Cuthrell, John Demme, Jane Harvey, Edward Kallman, Gene Laughery, Beverley Laughlin, Paul Lips, Vincent

Puccio, Jack McAlinden, Walt McGovern, David MacCurdy, John Moynahan, Dr. Stanley Mullin, Hal Taylor, George Ulich, George Walsh, Nancy Webb, and Dr. Joseph Zinkin. Their generous help has given this book a balance of viewpoints which work to increase its value to readers.

TIME IS
MONEY

CHAPTER 1

Should You Go on Your Own?

You may share the interest of many thoughtful men and women who are seriously exploring the question of going on their own in their professional life. They are looking for opportunities, revenue, and a more *satisfying* way to work. For example, you may want to consult, free-lance, or establish a profitable specialized service based on your personal qualifications and experience.

Helping you to accomplish this objective is one of the prime purposes of this book. In fact, just knowing that you can do it when *you* want to can give a wonderfully optimistic look to your future. Besides, who can tell what kinds of changes are ahead in your field? This book can give you a little "career insurance" that might come in handy at almost any time.

Like many of us, you may want to *ease* into professional independence on a part-time basis so that you can maintain reasonable levels of economic security as you move steadily ahead.

Interest in professional independence can come up quite naturally: for instance, if you are in an unpredictable and highly competitive specialty and are looking for ways to establish more control of your future; if you want to find dignified ways to develop additional revenue to offset inflation or the rising cost of educating a family; if you are heading for retirement and want to be active instead of bored; if your best efforts are meeting with bureaucratic indifference and you want to find a more satisfying way to work; if you have been looking for an opening only to find that everyone says that you are overqualified. These are a few typical situations where the urge toward professional independence can come up naturally. Then . . . there is your special reason right now.

You don't have to be a genius to get results or there wouldn't be so many solo operations around. You will need reasonable levels of knowledge and experience, some determination, and an appreciation of the spirit of adventure which is one of the most satisfying parts of taking control of your own future.

At this moment, you may not realize that you have what it takes because working on your own is different and hard to visualize from inside a salaried job. It is easy to overlook your strengths. For example, if you administer, manage, plan, design, create, solve problems, organize information, teach, sell, research, or do any of the jobs that have a direct impact on results in your field—you can be off and flying.

It is not unreasonable to suggest that *part* of what you know and do can be translated into a useful service that you can aim at a profitable marketplace . . . your personal marketplace.

The fact is that the qualifications for success are already in the hands of most professionals and specialists who work in fields like accounting, design, engineering, marketing, education, personnel, sales, financial services, publishing, communications, government services, business services, social and health services, the military, and dozens of other fields. They all depend on specialized knowledge and experience to keep them going.

What counts here is you and your field. Very likely it exists and prospers because of the ability of professionals and specialists to satisfy a marketplace. That's why what you do best in your daily work can offer you a practical and familiar starting point for professional independence. You can start naturally and move on from there. In fact, the book you now hold in your hands offers you most of the information you need to make your move really work.

While professional independence is a flexible idea whose time has come you can structure it your way. For example, you can start full- or part-time. You can concentrate on building a kind of economic security that you can control yourself. You can build toward your kind of objectives. A quiet, comfortable, and profitable professional service on your own terms? The start of a giant new organization? Maybe you would prefer something in between. The point is that you can decide.

You can also look ahead with a certain practical optimism. There are new levels of self-confidence that are doubly satisfying because you know that you have earned them. There is also a lot of self-respect contained in working steadily along with the purpose of building your own future. Tackling this job one step at a time makes the move both practical and workable. Many others have done it before. There is no reason why you can't do it successfully too.

Why Do People Go on Their Own?

Here are some answers given by professionals and specialists who have taken this step:

"I couldn't stand the big machine, they didn't understand what I was doing." From an engineer.

"I got tired of waiting for decisions that never came. I couldn't get any satisfaction from my job." From a social worker.

"I was too confined in the straightjacket of other people's thinking. I never got a real chance to try out my own." From a young manager.

"I got tired of having to explain everything I was doing three or four times." From a sales executive.

"I know my profession and I really want to do my work my way." From an editor.

"I got tired of responding to a bureaucracy and never being able to do what I was good at." From a teacher turned administrator.

"I want to have a strong and direct hand in what happens to me in the future. I don't think anyone else is looking." From a creative person.

"I had worked inside a giant corporation for years where all the important decisions are made in committees. I didn't know whether I was any good or not. I wanted to know, and that was my reason for going on my own." From a top management executive.

Here are some additional comments from thoughtful professionals and specialists that relate to their interest in professional independence.

J. T. is an economist with this idea: He thinks that decisions made by those amazing and anonymous wizards in the heart of the money mechanisms can cost a good woman or man a job in Scarsdale, Atlanta, Seattle, or Los Angeles. The results are often blandly billed as an "economic adjustment." It can be like having oblivion thrust upon you and can make an independent move necessary.

F. R. is a research scientist with this thought: "We live in an age of advanced technology which has developed an annoying habit of cutting out jobs and replacing them with new and different ones. There is a certain crushing impersonality about it all that stimulates interest in professional independence.

J. L. is a successful woman executive with this belief: Despite advances, there is evidence that women are passed over when the better jobs come up. Many of these women have superior knowledge and practical experience and would handle the added responsibilities more effectively. Frustration with this situation sparks interest in professional independence.

Two Keys to Success

If you make your move *on purpose*, you will start knowing that you really want the kind of independent, hard-working, and satisfying life that is often the result. If you are *pushed* into it by outside circumstances, you may have to struggle to overcome any natural resentment or anger which may have been generated by the situation you have left.

The first critical key to success is *wanting* to go on your own. This means wanting it seriously enough to make the day-to-day work interesting and to stimulate you to accept the necessity of adding to your skills to make it work. This is the opposite of making the move to *escape* from an unpleasant situation.

The second critical key to success is your determination to *build* solidly one step at a time. When you move toward professional independence with the determination to build, there is a strong impact on your morale and self-respect. Both work to help you get results.

Look for These Satisfactions

Starting out is an exciting experience to say the least. The very idea of striking out directly for your own professional and economic independence is genuinely satisfying. There is also the satisfaction of knowing that you are working *every day* to gain an increasing mastery of your own future—instead of leaving it to others who may not be paying attention.

There is special satisfaction and confidence available in taking responsibility for an assignment or project from the beginning through visible results and then getting paid for that work. Experience with this clear and direct work-results-revenue relationship can contribute a special kind of self-respect that can make you hard to beat in open competition.

You can expect to draw additional satisfaction from meeting and beating the challenges of learning new skills. Acquiring those new skills becomes easier when you see *in advance* that they will have a direct impact on the revenue and results you can get.

As you move ahead and gain momentum you can expect new satisfactions to crop up with each job well done. Hidden behind these satisfactions are two key factors: discipline and hard work. Both are needed to make your operation work smoothly. They are the source of the kind of steady performance that produces reliable results.

Move When You Are Ready

This is a good time to check on your viewpoint. Do you really want to go on your own now . . . or in the future? Can you see an opportunity to build if you make this move? If the idea has always appealed to you and that feeling has grown stronger and stronger, you may be a genuine candidate for a successful move.

But don't let this book or anyone else talk you into it. You are the sole judge. If you are favorably inclined . . . *do it when you are ready.* Being ready makes the move more natural and the initial steps work more smoothly.

The Real Substance

It comes down to six questions. Look them over and notice the balance they represent. That's why the first step in this approach is to gather information. First . . . the answers to these questions:

1. What is your offer of service? Developing that offer is the point and purpose of the next chapter.

2. Who is the real target for your service? A clear definition of your personal marketplace helps to make the move real rather than imaginary.

3. What will your offer of service cost you? There is help with this question in the chapter on pricing. Even so, you might be wise to draw in an accountant to help you. She or he can also tell you about relevant taxes that apply and other useful information.

4. How much will your offer of service cost your first client? There is information about estimating assignments and projects in

the chapter on pricing that will help you here. Again, you may want to draw on professional help from an accountant to be sure that you reflect your situation accurately when it comes to numbers and taxes.

5. Is your offer of service salable by you? This means is it simple, clear, and credible coming from one person? There is information in the chapter about selling that can help you with this problem.

6. Is your offer of service buyable by your prospects? Can they buy it without referring to other people in their organization? This can help you get quicker acceptance. There is information in the chapter on selling that will help you here, too.

The development of convincing answers to these questions can help you minimize risk and reduce your start-up time considerably.

Don't overlook friends and associates with specialized knowledge and experience who can contribute to the quality of your answers. You may be surprised at how willingly they will help. They are likely to admire your guts and privately envy the organized and determined way you are going about things.

The basic purpose is to reduce the time it takes to start up and develop sound sources of revenue. It pays to move one step at a time so that you can build solidly. Try to recognize clearly and beforehand the relationship between each step and the results you can get. This awareness can do wonders for your morale.

Two Big Differences

When you move from a regular salary with its implications of security to a situation where your income depends on someone paying your bills, money can take on a new sense of urgency. That's one big difference when you start out.

Money can produce unrealistic levels of worry which are additional and self-imposed pressures that can work against you. Try to *replace* that pressure with financial planning on an annual basis. This can put your financial picture into some perspective and may take some of the immediate pressure off.

The fact is that you have to get used to receiving your income in large chunks instead of every week or two. Sometimes, those large chunks add up to much more than your previous salary. With this in mind you may feel a bit less anxious about it all . . . so cheer up.

There are some things you can do about anxiety over money.

For instance, you can develop a clear annual overhead budget to tell you what you really need without any guesswork. Next, you can define a clear annual revenue target which is a point where you feel that you will be financially secure for the year. It is knowing when you arrive at that point that helps to reduce financial worry. The act of working toward that point can help you to avoid being intimidated by short-term financial pressure. Above all, don't let the *idea* of financial insecurity keep you from tackling the very problems that can help you to resolve it. After some practice it is quite possible to develop the revenue you need for a whole year in a matter of months.

There is specific information in the chapter on pricing that will show you how to establish a profitable price for your service and then develop annual revenue forecasts. Knowing what you are shooting for and when you reach it can do a lot to reduce unrealistic levels of financial concern. Start working on your financial future and you will see how it works.

When you work around the clock on a job where you initiate, respond, and react to different needs and requests from many sources, you are in a familiar routine for most professionals and specialists.

When you take the same specific actions on your own, with a price tag on your time, you will find a second major difference. You learn that *your* time is worth money on a very personal level. It takes a while to get used to this idea.

When you do, you may experience a change of viewpoint about work and the way you work. You may discover you have a tendency to try to get more done in less time than is realistic. It is a good time to determine to get a few things done really well rather than many things half done. The net results are a lot better.

The idea that your time is worth money is difficult to understand and apply after being on a salary. It can stimulate you to manage your time with increasing efficiency and ever more satisfying results.

How Long Does It Take?

This will depend on your situation and starting point. It will also depend on how effectively and consistently you work at making things happen. For instance, if you move from your job with an assignment from a new client you can start immediately. If you develop assignments from your present employer you are off and running. If neither of these paths is open to you, it can take 18 months or more to become reasonably well established. You can develop revenue before then, of course.

Why does it take so long? It is often because many professionals and specialists know *their* work but are not familiar with how to operate on their own. One of the prime purposes of this book is to help you to substantially reduce the start-up period.

Many critical needs with which you may not be familiar have a direct bearing on results. The information needed to establish a fair price for your service is one. The ability to sell your own service is another. When these steps don't work effectively, there can be long waits for acceptance. This can account for the 18 months. Remember, your prospects may not be in a hurry just when you are. This also accounts for delays in getting results. All this throws a sharp focus on the need for careful advance planning to achieve early acceptance.

What Does It Cost?

This varies from one individual to another. You will make choices that influence the cost. For instance, if you start at home with minimum overhead you can cut your start-up costs dramatically. If you move in with friends, work out of their office and exchange your services for rent, you can also cut your costs. If, on the other hand, you open lavish offices with secretarial and staff help you will not only increase your start-up costs and financial risks but you will feel additional pressure to develop early revenue.

At a minimum it is wise to carefully evaluate what you really need to open up so that you can develop effective cost control from the beginning.

You can estimate some minimum costs by deciding where you want to start—at home, in an office shared with friends, at rented desk space, or by opening your own office. There is more information about start-up costs in Chapter 3 which can help you stay on solid ground.

You can expect some basic costs. You will need telephone service, a telephone answering machine or service, some stationery and supplies, and your own working equipment. You may have most of that equipment already. This can keep your investment down to a few hundred dollars or less which makes starting up practical for most professionals or specialists.

What Is the Earning Potential?

While this depends on what you do and the value that clients or customers see in what you do, it is also a fact that many professional and specialized services operate on a time basis. This can give you an idea of income potential. You will also find that many of these services operate on the basis of assignments, jobs, or projects. They plan on the basis of billable days in a year. You can do the same.

For example, if you charge $50 an hour and successfully bill 100 seven-hour days in a year you will earn a gross income of $35,-000. If you charge $100 an hour and bill 100 seven-hour days in a year you will earn a gross income of $70,000. As you will see in the chapter on pricing, it takes time to develop a service where you can bill as much as 200 days in one year.

For your own planning purposes, you can put in your own hourly rate, multiply it by the number of seven-hour billable days you expect, and get some idea of your earning potential in one year.

Earning power is always subject to many factors. Some are: the quality and consistency of the performance; the number and caliber of genuine prospects; the reliability of the business relationships. Don't be intimidated. Others have done this and so can you. It pays to move one step at a time. It also helps to have some way to project your earning power as part of your early planning. It can help you to determine whether or not this move will be worth it to you from a financial viewpoint.

Establish Your Current Financial Position

If you define your personal financial picture on an annual basis you will get a clearer and more reliable idea of what your needs really are.

To be complete, your financial information should cover your assets, liabilities, income sources, fixed and variable expenses. You may find some of this information handy in last year's checkbook and from other sources that reflect your special situation.

This information can help you in several ways. You can establish a practical budget for your personal expenses in line with your clearly defined financial needs. You can also define a reasonable annual revenue goal to cover those needs. With this information and a definition of your total assets in hand you may also be able to sketch the amount of start-up time you can *afford*.

Each of the following charts suggests some standard items as reminders. What counts is your special financial facts which are different. Just take out the items that don't apply to you and add those that will give you a factual picture.

What Are Your Total Assets?

In short: what do you own? Some standard items are listed here with room to put down dollar amounts. Just jot down your special facts and drop any that don't fit.

Reminders: House. Stocks. Bonds. Land. Car. Jewelry. Paintings. Furniture. Antiques. Gold and silver objects. Insurance policies. Savings account.

ITEM	AMOUNT
1. _____	$ _____
2. _____	$ _____
3. _____	$ _____
4. _____	$ _____
5. _____	$ _____
6. _____	$ _____
7. _____	$ _____
8. _____	$ _____
9. _____	$ _____
10. _____	$ _____
11. _____	$ _____
12. _____	$ _____
13. _____	$ _____
14. _____	$ _____
15. _____	$ _____
Total of what you own	$ _____

What Are Your Liabilities?

Here's another way to put it: What do you owe? Some standard items are listed here as reminders. Put in your special facts and add them up.

Reminders: Mortgage loan. Personal loans. Business loans. Automobile loans. Educational loans. Installment loan for appliances or other items.

ITEM	AMOUNT
1. _____	$ _____
2. _____	$ _____
3. _____	$ _____
4. _____	$ _____
5. _____	$ _____
6. _____	$ _____
7. _____	$ _____
8. _____	$ _____
9. _____	$ _____
10. _____	$ _____
11. _____	$ _____
12. _____	$ _____
13. _____	$ _____
14. _____	$ _____
15. _____	$ _____
Total of what you owe	$ _____

What Is Your Annual Income?

Here are some different sources of income as a reminder. Fill in your special story below.

Reminders: Your spouse's salary. Dividends. Interest. Income from rent, a trust, a pension, social security, commissions for past service, or royalties from past work.

ITEM	AMOUNT
1. _____	$ _____
2. _____	$ _____
3. _____	$ _____
4. _____	$ _____
5. _____	$ _____
6. _____	$ _____
7. _____	$ _____
8. _____	$ _____
9. _____	$ _____
10. _____	$ _____
11. _____	$ _____
12. _____	$ _____
13. _____	$ _____
14. _____	$ _____
15. _____	$ _____
Your total annual income before taxes	$ _____

What Are Your Fixed Annual Expenses?

This means expenses that you know you must pay each month . . . each quarter . . . or annually. Some standard items are listed here. Your own checkbook will probably show you what you need here.

Reminders: Rent or mortgage payment. Property insurance. Auto insurance. Health insurance. Home telephone, heating, and electrical. Installment payments.

ITEM	MONTHLY	ANNUAL
1. _____	$ _____	$ _____
2. _____	$ _____	$ _____
3. _____	$ _____	$ _____
4. _____	$ _____	$ _____
5. _____	$ _____	$ _____
6. _____	$ _____	$ _____
7. _____	$ _____	$ _____
8. _____	$ _____	$ _____
9. _____	$ _____	$ _____
10. _____	$ _____	$ _____
11. _____	$ _____	$ _____
12. _____	$ _____	$ _____
13. _____	$ _____	$ _____
14. _____	$ _____	$ _____
15. _____	$ _____	$ _____

Your total annual fixed expenses $ _____

What Are Your Variable Expenses?

These are expenses that keep changing. You still have to pay them but you can only estimate them. Take a look at last year's checkbook for some facts. Include the unexpected expenses as well to give your estimate special reliability.

Reminders: Food. Clothing. Entertainment. Home repair. Auto repair. Vacations. Special medical or dental treatment. Home improvements. Furniture. Appliances.

ITEM	AMOUNT
1. _____	$ _____
2. _____	$ _____
3. _____	$ _____
4. _____	$ _____
5. _____	$ _____
6. _____	$ _____
7. _____	$ _____
8. _____	$ _____
9. _____	$ _____
10. _____	$ _____
11. _____	$ _____
12. _____	$ _____
13. _____	$ _____
14. _____	$ _____
15. _____	$ _____

An estimate of your total annual variable expenses $ _____

Your Personal Financial Picture

This will give you an idea of where you stand for planning purposes. Put your annual tax bills in here so that you can see more clearly exactly what you have to spend each year as of now.

The total of what you own	$ _____	
The total of what you owe	$ _____	
What you are worth		$ _____
Your annual income *before* taxes	$ _____	
Your annual tax bills	$ _____	
What you have to spend		$ _____
Your total annual fixed expenses	$ _____	
Your total annual variable expenses	$ _____	
What you need now		$ _____

How to Use Your Financial Facts

Use financial facts as planning tools to help keep your start-up program on an economically realistic basis. Let the facts help you decide where you should trim your sails. Use them to recognize sources of capital that can give you additional start-up time and flexibility during the first steps. Your financial facts can also help you develop a practical budget for investing in necessary materials, equipment, supplies, and services you will need. Look them over with the idea of making the best possible use of your resources to avoid economic pressure as much as possible and give yourself the time you need to accomplish the first steps.

Sources of Start-up Funds

Start-up funds are resources that can be translated into cash for your short-term needs during the first stages. Here are some examples:

1. The loan value of an insurance policy. Insurance companies charge the lowest interest rates. With a loan from this source you can still keep your insurance in force.

2. A bank loan against a savings account can develop short-term operating funds and still keep your savings intact.

3. The liquidation of unused property such as land, automobiles, houses, or other valuable property that you can turn into working capital.

4. The development of a loan based on valuables which are used as collateral. Land, paintings, gold, bonds, and other easily liquidated property can produce start-up funds that will buy more time for you.

5. The placing of a mortgage on property and on the equipment you need to work with can produce cash. An expensive piece of professional equipment can be mortgaged to give you short-term funds while you still have the equipment available for use.

Awareness of potential sources of funds can give you economic confidence that can be very helpful during the first stages. Take another look at your financial picture to get a clear idea of sources of capital that can give you maximum time to start. You may never need to use these sources but knowing they are there can really help.

Can a Commercial Banker Help You?

The answer to the above question is a highly qualified "yes." The qualifications consist of your answers to a banker's questions. This is what a banker will want to know: What do you want the money for? How long will you need it? When and how are you going to pay it back? How much are you going to invest yourself? What is your personal financial picture showing assets and liabilities? What is your anticipated revenue and profit for the first and second years? What kind of collateral do you have to secure a loan? The banker is likely to want *more* than the amount of the loan in terms of collateral. It will have to be easily liquidated like stocks, bonds, or the content of your savings account.

Bankers think that a small loan is somewhere in the area of $50,000. Positive results can depend on the financial climate and money supplies when you want the loan. When banks have plenty of money to loan they may be interested in you. Your best chances are likely to be with a bank where you are known and where you are planning to establish your operations. If you and your financial information are well organized a banker will be impressed. If you are also qualified and determined, your banker may experience a change of viewpoint. He or she may begin to see you as an opportunity.

Your banker might say: "This is only the beginning. There is the possibility of future business and contacts."

It will take seven to ten working days to process your application. A small loan in situations like this takes more work to process than those with established organizations. The idea of this "more work" can turn some bankers away from you for other more profitable opportunities. Most bankers are conservative and they won't make loans which may bring them problems inside the bank. This is another source of possible reluctance.

Once your application is accepted, the banker may get in touch with a computerized credit service. Your name, address, place of business, and social security number will go into a computer and a coded print-out will come out. It will show each bank or finance company where you have done business, your credit status (delinquent or current), and the number of times you have been delinquent in the past. If you pass this test and the banker is interested, your chances of getting a loan will go up. This brief review of the process of developing a bank loan aims at helping you to determine whether you want to try this direction or not.

Build an Economic Bridge

Here are some ways to make a transition, maintain some income, and still have free time to start up.

1. Translate *part* of your present job into occasional or continuing assignments from your present employer after you leave. This arrangement has to work well for both you and your employer. Take a look for part-time assignments in your job or department and see if you can make this approach produce for you. Here are some examples:

J. D. is a technical writer. She built a bridge by taking over certain time-consuming and highly technical writing assignments for her company from the outside. They needed this work done and it was easier for them to accept her suggestion than find someone else whom they would have to pay full-time. It worked for her and it gave her free time to get started on her own.

F. C. is a young architect. He took over several specific design assignments that relieved pressure on senior partners in his firm. It worked for him because it worked for them.

J. M. took over certain research jobs for his marketing firm. This saved time for other staff members who were then free for more important work. Examine your situation for an opportunity like this. Perhaps you can define a small or specific piece of your work that you can offer to handle from the outside. Make a clear proposition to your employers with a price tag so that your suggestion is buyable.

This approach can work particularly well when the assignment consists of something you do well that other people in your company or organization don't want to handle themselves. If they know they need it and don't want to get involved themselves, you may be looking at a really good opportunity.

You have to identify the content of the assignment yourself and then make the proposition. They may want to change it to suit themselves or adjust your price a bit. Fine! Your real objective is to develop some revenue-producing activity and get some free time for yourself.

2. Can you sell one or two days a week to your employer or another organization in your field? You may be able to arrange this while you are in your present job. This can also give you an economic bridge and some free time. You can start this approach with the advantage of knowing some of the needs and may be able to identify specific areas of activity where you could be of maximum value. It is important to define what you will do and then let them decide. During an exploratory conversation you may be able to find out more about the situation as they see it and adjust your offer accordingly. You may be able to help them avoid hiring a new or full-time staff member. If this is in the picture, you can attract their interest and attention right away.

J. D. is a public relations specialist. She offered to prepare feature articles for certain manufacturing firms in her area. She confined her activity to the research and preparation of feature articles only. This work took two days a week and left her free for planning and preparation of her own service.

3. Can you develop a part-time job? This is another practical way to get some free time. With this approach you quickly and frankly move into the part-time job market to produce revenue and still get some time to build your service.

4. Can you develop an assignment or series of assignments from your first client while you are in your present job? If your situation makes this possible, it is an effective way to get started. However, it may not be available at the outset. Hence, other choices suggested

here may be more practical on a short-term basis. Select the most practical economic bridge you see and concentrate on making it work for you as soon as possible.

A Cheerful Thought

Most of the biggest names in American business, industry, and many professional and specialized services were once just ideas in the heads of determined people who wanted to do their things their way. The vast majority started alone or quite small. Many were unknown, unloved (economically), and began with the idea of wanting to build something of their own, using a new approach based on their knowledge and experience ... their viewpoints and ideas ... their way of doing things. If you feel in this kind of mood, you may be a candidate for success on your own.

CHAPTER 2

Package Your Knowledge and Experience for Sale

This chapter offers an organized approach to translating your knowledge and experience into a custom-tailored service aimed at a specific marketplace. Emphasis is on close-at-hand sources of information that can help you build solidly. There are trouble spots to avoid. You can move a step at a time to maintain control and stay on solid ground. The objective is a self-sufficient service based on your strengths that you can price and sell on your own. You will find ways to define your new service. You can evaluate your service to help you decide whether it will be profitable and salable. There are tests to help you reduce risks before you invest too much of your own time or money.

Why Start a Custom-tailored Service?

By offering a custom-tailored service, you can use the hard-won knowledge and practical experience that make you valuable in the first place. Running your own service gives you maximum self-sufficiency, dignity, and control.

You may share the feelings of many professionals and specialists who are loyal to their work and trust their own experience. You may also feel that it is out of character for you to start a business in the popular sense of buying a food franchise, a laundromat, or a motel.

Equally important, your development of a service that capitalizes on your own skills guarantees you continued use of your best qualifications. You can avoid the intense frustration that can come when you have to put aside your most familiar and successful activities to learn a new field. In some instances, it may come down to this: What else can a good salesman do but continue to sell? What else can a good architect do but continue to design? What else can a good teacher do but continue to teach? The same is true of most professionals and specialists with a stake in their experience.

You can custom-tailor your service in two senses: (1) the content can be solidly based on what you do best to give you firm and reliable confidence; (2) the content can be tailored to the needs of a specific marketplace to make it salable. By recognizing and working both sides of this "coin'" you can build with greater expectation of realistic and reliable results.

Establish Reasonable Control

Give yourself as much freedom as possible to develop your service idea. Try to avoid inhibitions that can work against you. Here are some examples:

If you have moved from an unfavorable job climate, try to avoid the natural urge to "show them." This isn't easy. But the fact is that they are not looking.

Try to avoid preconceived ideas and judgments as much as possible. Sometimes there is an irresistible urge to say to yourself "that won't work" when you don't really know. Only the marketplace would know! It is impossible to develop good ideas and edit them at the same time. Judging is a second step.

Flatly refuse to entertain the idea that your knowledge and experience *won't* yield a good service idea just because you can't see it at first. Your thoughts are likely to be vague and general at the beginning. Have patience.

Sometimes, you may have a feeling beforehand that your resulting idea must be *perfect*, that it must somehow demonstrate uniqueness, brilliance, or prestige. Such preconceived ideas can easily block out your discovery of what you want. Recognize that formulating your idea will take patience, digging, and a reasonable length of time. With this in mind, it is important to *do it your way.*

Stay Away from Frustration

Excessive modesty can defeat you. Sheer egotism will produce nothing more than an expensive ego trip. Get out of these trouble spots by concentrating on accumulating reliable information from which you can develop your service idea.

Thinking totally in terms of yourself and what you want will often lead to frustration. Questions like What do I want?, Where do I fit?, and How much money can I make? are certainly valid. But they don't belong in an objective evaluation of your background with the purpose of developing a salable service. In fact, try to avoid self-seeking as much as possible to get a clear picture of the facts.

Remember, the success of your service depends in part on its content and quality. But it also depends very substantially on acceptance in your marketplace. Your prospective clients have the final decision. Your self-interest won't cut much ice with them and can work against you at this early stage by blocking out the recognition and development of facts and information you need to evaluate your background thoroughly and effectively.

Remember the famous Edsel car? Certainly the people at Ford thought it was "right" when they produced it. But their prospects disagreed. The car never did catch on. It is encouraging to remember that the confident people at Ford promptly picked themselves up again and started some really beautiful new car ideas that were successful because they *did* satisfy the market.

Getting a good service idea and testing it out may be something like this. It is practical to develop your own service idea or adapt one to your needs. You can visualize and develop it and then show it to prospects to find out what they need or want. Then you can make adjustments that fit your service more precisely to the marketplace you want to cultivate. This is a step-by-step way to develop a service idea with minimum risk.

Three Custom-tailored Services

You will notice that each of the services described below started from a different point: one from exploring the needs of a defined marketplace; another from knowledge and practical experience; the third from noticing a problem shared by a large group.

F. P. is a real estate specialist in England. He started his service from the needs of a specific marketplace. They are small castle owners. He established a service to promote small castles as tourist attractions. His service helps owners to meet rising maintenance and tax costs. He uses his knowledge and experience to the hilt. He provides an interesting new attraction for tourists.

J. C. knows how to write about equipment and machinery. He

had done it for years in all media for an advertising agency. When he lost his job he found that this extensive background was almost "too much" when it came to earning revenue. He frequently heard the word "overqualified." He established a service by using *part* of his knowledge and experience: his ability to plan, research, and write technical articles. He picked a specific marketplace: the public relations directors of computer systems companies. He found about twenty of them in his area. They were more than enough to get him started.

By confining his service to one activity (the writing of technical articles) he made his "puzzling background" specific, clear, and salable. By concentrating on one market and its special needs he made his service relevant and realistic. By establishing a clear hourly rate he made his service buyable. Within one year he developed more than enough income to maintain his family with a modest surplus.

J. K. is a university professor whose specialty ran out of students. She has top credentials as a teacher of French language, history, and literature. She also has some business experience managing investments. She draws on years of living, studying, and working in Paris and other European cities. She started by taking note of the problems that American executives face when they work with French executives.

She found a widely recognized communications gap as well as large gaps in culture and tradition worked against mutual understanding and an easy business relationship. She responded by offering a practical seminar covering sensitive topics which aim at making French executives and their customs and traditions clear to American executives doing business in France. She stayed in character. She continued to use her knowledge, experience, and teaching talent. She uncovered and capitalized on a need that was recognized in many multinational corporations that send teams of specialists to work for them in France. She had a real winner.

These three examples of successful services illustrate the point that a practical service idea can start almost anywhere.

You can find one by exploring and packaging a piece of your knowledge. Your idea may appear when you examine your practical experience. Maybe a combination of knowledge and practical experience will produce what you want. A good idea can also come from your identification and exploration of a specific marketplace. Don't overlook your recognition of a common problem which you are qualified to help resolve. You will notice that these sources are close at hand and within easy reach so that you can take action now.

The service idea you want is there! The real problem is uncovering or discovering it. Let's begin by looking at some promising sources. Then you can pick a starting point that suits you and fits your background.

Start with Your Knowledge

We are looking for a piece of your knowledge that can produce visible results. Remember J. C., the advertising man? He had plenty of background preparing all kinds of advertising material. But he plucked out a *piece* of his knowledge and experience: the planning, research, and writing of technical articles. That piece made his broad background specific, clear, salable, and buyable for purposes of starting his service. You can do the same thing.

But you may have to look hard because the "piece" you want may be something you take for granted, a chunk that you don't think is particularly valuable because it seems so ordinary to you. Just because something is easy for you doesn't mean that everyone else can do it either as easily or as well.

Do you have a piece of knowledge that involves subject material that you like and that comes *naturally* to you? Maybe you're marvelous with numbers . . . words . . . a certain kind of problem . . . industry . . . or technique. This kind of background can put you in a strong position. Why? Because you can *do it* easily, you will be able to deliver results easily, and this can help you beat competition.

The piece you are looking for may be large or small. But it is specific and can produce visible results for a defined marketplace—one that is large, elite, local, specialized, international (as you see fit) but one that is sophisticated about your kind of service and profitable. Being specific about your knowledge can provide you with a solid basis for starting your service. Let's take a look at some examples.

An engineer with extensive experience planning and directing major bridge-building projects found that this broad background was not salable coming from one person. He discovered a salable piece in his knowledge of how to evaluate soil conditions for foundation work. He turned this piece into a profitable consulting service aimed at engineering and architectural firms which did not have this specialty on staff because they didn't need it often enough. This approach may be a good starting point for you. Can you package your knowledge to sell to *other services* in your field? When you name some of those services you may be looking at a useful target. It is a natural starting point for many knowledge-based services.

A personnel specialist with broad experience establishing personnel policy and benefit programs found that she couldn't sell this comprehensive background. So she packaged this piece: her knowledge of how to set up a benefit program. She created a service for small companies interested in starting such programs on a modest scale. She had been there before, which made her service convincing and helped her to sell it.

A public relations man with financial background and effective media contacts found that this only made him look like everyone else in his field. He packaged his knowledge to focus it on the needs of company presidents who wanted to attract new investors. This choice of a narrow target made his knowledge relevant and clear to prospects. It made him buyable rather than general and vague. This choice also enabled him to determine which *parts* of his knowledge he needed to perform this specific job.

An editor with extensive knowledge of science and technology discovered in that knowledge the basis for a successful service. She knew how to develop technical book ideas and a range of authors who could write them. She set up a service developing book ideas and finding authors for them. She sold this package to selected publishers—her marketplace. She used her knowledge to produce visible results that she could sell. She also had the satisfaction of doing her work her way.

As you can see, the purpose is to avoid broad and vague offers of service which are hard to sell. A specific piece of knowledge can be "understandable" as a starting point for your service. It can also make that service credible and believable coming from you. If knowledge is your strong point, this approach to packaging it may be just what you have been looking for.

Start with Your Practical Experience

Practical experience is different from knowledge and deserves your special attention. It is a reliable source of information, observations, facts, and judgments which may produce a solid basis for a realistic service.

For instance, an unusually effective administrator with a real talent for organization and the handling of administrative detail took this approach. She noticed from her experience that many people in sales hate paperwork. She packaged her talent and aimed it at the principals of small service organizations who have a constant need to sell their services but don't have the time to organize their information to do that job well. Her service helped them to develop prospect lists, organize selling material, set up appointments, schedule follow-up calls, prepare call reports, and handle key correspondence. Her service idea came from her experience watching sales executives struggle with paperwork. Her service idea was a smashing success.

Many professionals and specialists move around working on assignments for different clients or customers. This experience can produce good results, too. Is there an idea waiting for you in your experience working with customers or clients?

Here's an example. A retired bank officer who frequently visited customers' offices and plants noticed how much the executives of smaller companies had to struggle to develop the information they needed to qualify for a bank loan. He established a service that prepared bank loan applications on an hourly rate basis. Then he found that his clients wanted him to negotiate the loans. Within a year he had developed more than eighty clients among small company presidents in a twenty-five-mile radius of his home. He needed such a large number because the problem is infrequent in many smaller companies. But with eighty clients he kept busy, interested, solvent, and enjoyed the self-respect and satisfaction of continuing to use his experience.

Package Part of Your Job

Can you turn part of your job into a service? This is another close-at-hand starting point. You may find that "the whole thing" is hard to cope with and a piece might be easier to handle.

Here's an example. A financial specialist who spent part of her working time making up reports on the financial condition of overseas subsidiaries in France, Germany, and Japan couldn't see any value in this part of her job—at first. Then she realized that she had a great deal of knowledge and experience with economic conditions in France. She used this part of her job to start her service. She aimed it at financial executives in U.S. companies with business interests in France. She lives in New York City. She was a bit surprised to find more than four hundred companies that "qualified for her service" within a five-block area in midtown Manhattan. They became her marketplace. She provides them with monthly reports on current economic conditions in France with emphasis on selected factors that influence monetary rates. She started by packaging part of her job. Once she got started, she found that she needed to amend her own background with new information to make her service increasingly interesting to her clients and more comprehensive. You can do the same thing if you feel it is necessary.

A product manager used part of his job as the basis for his service. In the course of his work, he managed sales, finance, product development, advertising, and personnel. He was also responsible for profit levels on an important packaged product. He chose the "product development" part of his job as his starting point. This choice was supported by his experience in marketing, sales, advertising, and finance. He established a specialized service which created, developed, designed, and tested new product ideas. The net results were sold to major manufacturers in his field who became his personal marketplace. This is unusually complex for a starting point. It might be better to keep things simpler. But it illustrates how you can use part of your job as the basis for starting your service.

An ambitious young sales and service engineer decided that she couldn't wait out the long climb to the top of her company. She had a lot of field experience solving maintenance problems on computer equipment and calming down complaining customers. She recognized that fixing the equipment was one thing but that fixing complaining customers so they wouldn't spread "the bad word" about her company and products was another. She realized that she had a talent: keeping customers happy . . . turning complainers into believers. She established a service to train other service engineers in the fine art of handling complainers and turning them into boosters again. She sold this service to equipment sales managers in her area in the form of a four-hour presentation that really got everyone stirred up. She was using "what comes naturally" as the basis of her service. Maybe you can do the same thing.

Explore One Market

Here is another approach to finding a service idea that may work well for you. Select a market where they will greet you as "one of us" from a professional viewpoint; people doing your kind of work where you already know and understand some of *their* needs and problems; your opposite number with other organizations, for instance; people you believe will put genuine value on your kind of knowledge and experience and where there is some evidence that they would be able to pay a fair price for it. Set up ten or twelve separate interviews with people who have business or professional needs you could satisfy. You are there to identify a specific need that could be the basis of your service because you don't want to waste time with guesswork and want some "input" to work with. You can expand this approach to several entirely different kinds of groups—wherever you feel there may be a real opportunity that you want to explore.

J. R. did this by picking out an elite group of sales executives with responsibility for the management of national sales teams of more than a thousand members. He had done this himself so he knew what it was like. He developed a set of questions to "smoke out" some of the current needs and problems of his personal "test market." His questions were of the earthy "what, who, where, when, why'" variety which have a refreshing way of producing usable answers. When his peers found out that he was going on his own and sincerely seeking information (not trying to sell something) they were delighted to talk with him. He took careful notes for use later on. He made a point of approaching each interview with an open mind and the idea of looking for something they needed and wanted that he could deliver on his own. He found that they had a lot of basic problems in common: the inadequacy of market research; the translation of market research into usable sales material; a sound way to respond to short-term competitive pricing tactics. He also found that they were intensely curious about *each other*. They wanted to know what "the other fellow" was doing about some of "my" problems. This came through in several interviews and struck J. R. as just right for him. He developed an elite series of conferences based on sharing solutions to common problems. His "test market" became his first participants and continuing boosters.

You May Be Surprised

When people in a marketplace find that you are sincerely seeking information and not trying to sell them something, you may be surprised and delighted at how graciously many will receive and talk with you. In fact, you may get a lot more information than you bargained for once things get rolling. Let it come. You can never tell when something spontaneous might strike you as "just right" or help you identify the service idea you are looking for.

Take along written questions focused on bringing out information, ideas, and judgments about what they are doing . . . what they want short-term ... what they want to accomplish long-term. Ask about some of the problems they see ahead. When you start by telling them that you are frankly looking for information and objective judgment because you want to go on your own, they are likely to be interested. They may also admire the organized way you are doing things. Don't be surprised if some of them ask you to keep in touch and let them know how it works out. You may be talking to your first clients. Who knows?

Define Your Service

The next step is to define your service as simply as you can at this early stage. Define it from four viewpoints:

1. The background of knowledge and/or experience that forms the basis of your service.
2. What your service does for your marketplace.
3. The specific marketplace you are aiming at.
4. The first rough daily rate or price you would charge. (The pricing chapter in this book can help you make certain that your service is going to be profitable.)

Here are some examples:

From a geologist: "My service is based on extensive knowledge of and practical experience with the development of mineral resources in the states of Colorado, Wyoming, and Idaho. The service enables owners or potential investors in mining properties in these states to evaluate specific property before investing in its development. The service is available on a per diem basis plus expenses."

From a teacher: "My service is based on my knowledge of and practical experience as a teacher of reading. It enables personnel and human resources management in corporations to establish a program to improve the reading skills of staff members. The service is available on the basis of a per student charge."

From a market researcher: "My service is based on experience doing market research for business service organizations. The service enables accounting firms to analyze and develop practical new markets custom-tailored to them ... their situations ... their resources. The service is available on a per diem basis plus expenses."

From a law professor: "My service is based on the specific needs of foreign investors seeking real estate properties in Chicago. The service is based on my knowledge of current offerings and particularly of the steps required to complete a major transaction in Chicago. It is an information service made available through banks to improve their relationships with important foreign customers. It is available on a per diem basis plus expenses."

The purpose here is to crystallize your service idea and define it on paper in a preliminary form—to move it from being an abstract idea to becoming a concrete expression that you can develop and refine. This first definition step will also help you understand what it is yourself and avoid generalities and vagueness. Once it is safely on paper you can work on it until it becomes real to you. It may haunt you for a while. You have to get used to it yourself first. If it holds up, you may become convinced that you really have a good thing!

Service ideas are abstract and a lot depends on the ability of your marketplace to "get" your message. Professional and specialized services are frequently purchased and used by people who are unfamiliar with their content. It is also a fact that most people have trouble understanding abstractions but won't admit it. This throws a sharp focus on the need for simplicity, directness, and clarity.

Since a really good service idea is simple it can often be stated simply. Some can be "talked" with reasonable expectation that the talk will be understood. Others need to be visualized to make them clear. Visualizing your service makes it "real" to people and you can "show" as well as "tell." This can be particularly helpful with people who would rather look than listen.

Here are some ways to visualize your service. The purpose is to show what your service *does* . . . or what your service enables your prospective client to do. This is different from defining how it works. Most people don't want to know what makes the wheels go round.

Have you ever asked a professional or specialist (with a service you are unfamiliar with) these questions: What do you do? How does your service help me? Where does it fit? What are your credentials? Answers to these questions can help make the visualization of your service convincing.

Give the visualization of your service a title. For instance, you have a program for executives doing business in France. Start with a title that tells them what you are going to be talking about. Then use specific material that shows what your service does and/or what your service enables your prospects to do or accomplish. The whole thing may be just a few pages but they can make your service real to you and your prospects.

Here are some more content suggestions for review. Pick out those that fit your situation or develop your own.

CASE HISTORIES. They are favorites because they can show the problem, what was done, and what happened.

EXAMPLES. Specific examples of work that directly relates your service to your prospective client's interests and needs are excellent.

EDITORIAL. Sometimes you can find editorial material that directly supports the need for your service. This evidence from a third party might take up a couple of pages.

CREDENTIALS. Your own background for performing the work will be helpful. A page of material about selected knowledge and experience which supports the quality of your service will be interesting and convincing to prospects.

PROBLEM SOLUTIONS. This is another way to show what your service does and where it fits. The use of photographs (before and after) can help to make this kind of material clear and interesting.

STATISTICS. People like to look at graphs and other factual material. Perhaps you can use statistics to show results.

FACTS. This means facts about the kinds of problems you can help to solve. Facts from the marketplace. Facts from your knowledge and experience. Facts that demonstrate the need. A solid basis of fact will make your visualization of your service all the more convincing.

DEMONSTRATION. This is the most powerful way to "show" your service. It is not always practical, but if you can demonstrate your service, you will stand out from the crowd.

This preliminary visualization of your service can make it real both to you and your prospective clients and give you something to work with when you test your service.

You may also want to use it to see if you can raise funds to help you through the start-up period. It need not be elaborate. Often, a simple presentation book (the kind you buy in a stationery store) is all that's needed to put the material in sequence for easy review.

Reduce Risks with This Analysis

It pays to be candid with yourself and do a little more digging to make certain that your service idea has maximum opportunity for success. Here are five questions that can help you test the practicality of your service.

1. Is your service practical and deliverable by you? Consider this point carefully. Is the service you have visualized convincing and believable coming from one person? Can you yourself deliver what you promise (or with minimum outside help)? Would you buy it yourself?

2. What will your service cost you in out-of-pocket dollars? You can arrive at this figure by itemizing your costs. You may want to get some help from an accountant. But as clear an answer to this question as possible will help to keep you profitable from the beginning.

3. What will your service cost your first client? This may have to be simply a believable estimate until you get a client and try it out. But come as close as you can. This can also help you determine or forecast your future income to some extent.

4. Is your service salable by you? Take into account the time and economic resources available when you start. It can boil down to sending some letters and calling for appointments. But it pays to check on this point to make certain that your service idea is salable and convincing coming from you.

5. Is your service buyable by your specific prospects? Some services can be purchased only by certain people at certain levels. It pays to analyze your prospects in advance to make sure that they can buy your service on their own. The point is simply to avoid the "waiting around" that comes when the approval of purchase has to go through a chain of command where it can easily disappear.

If your service holds up reasonably well through this evaluation it is time for the next step.

Define Your Marketplace

Make certain that the prospects in your marketplace are in a sound and realistic position to be interested in and buy your service. This is another brief check to help you get all the advantages you can. Can you confine your prospects to areas where you have a solid chance of liking the subject and enjoying the day-to-day work? Consider the caliber of the people. Would you be able to work comfortably with them? Good personal "chemistry" can be critical to the satisfactory delivery of professional services. Few relationships are perfect, but keeping chemistry in mind can help you later on.

Evaluate the continuity of need for your service in a given marketplace. The presence of continuity can help you develop a service where long-term relationships are possible. This quality can make your service more profitable for you and more convenient for your future clients or customers. Aim at a marketplace that you can reach easily and economically. Sometimes physical convenience can both save your time and also encourage acceptance of your service. Now for the next step.

Tailor Your Service

This means test it *outside*, in your marketplace, so that you can tailor it to specific needs. This is where you can use the visualization of your service if you like. Establish a "test panel" of ten or twelve real prospects. They are the only people in the world who can tell you whether you have a winner or not . . . or how to fix what you have to make it a winner.

Tell them that you are trying to determine the feasibility of a new service idea that might be of interest to them. Ask if they would take a look. Take along a set of questions. Show your visualization. Ask them the questions. Take careful notes and concentrate on getting their exact words. Write up each call carefully and build up a file of these reports. Ask the same questions of everyone. You will probably find that a pattern of similar answers develops. When there is agreement you may well find reliable reasons to make adjustments. You are looking for reliable evidence from real prospects to help you evaluate your service and adjust it (if necessary) to give it maximum interest and value . . . to help you get early acceptance. Here are some "test" questions for your review. You may want to adapt some of them to your special situation and add others. These are just to help you get started.

1. What is your attitude toward this kind of service? People's attitudes influence their impressions, which are sometimes lasting. Your knowledge of their attitudes can help you add convincing qualities to your service and your sales program.

2. What special needs would this kind of service fill for you? You may discover some uses for your service that hadn't occurred to you.

3. What are the five most important benefits and advantages you see in this kind of service? These are important reasons why your prospects will buy your service. The ideas of real prospects in their own words can give you an immediate insight into selling your market. They might even come up with ideas you can use right away.

4. How would you justify the use of this kind of service? Answers to this question give you another opportunity to focus on prospects' needs as they see them. They may also tell you whether or not they use outside services.

5. How would you justify the cost of this kind of service? This question can produce information about their ideas regarding the dollar value of your kind of service which can serve as a guideline to you in pricing.

6. What are the three most important values you see in this kind of service? Your knowledge of their ideas of value can help you improve the quality of your service and enhance your chances of early acceptance.

7. What are the three most practical reasons why you would buy this service? Solid answers to this question may be reworked and included in your sales presentation later, or at least they may help convince you of the validity of your service as nothing else can.

8. What would you expect from this kind of service? Answers to this question can help you find out what they want in terms of personal service. Again, you may be able to improve the content and quality of your service.

9. What is the most important satisfaction this service should deliver from your viewpoint? Remember, people buy their idea of satisfaction as long as they also believe they are getting their money's worth. These answers may also be incorporated into your presentation of your service.

Use the results of this "outside test" to tailor your service in order to make the content more useful and your service more salable.

You may have other questions about content, price, delivery, and other specifics that will make your service successful. Don't forget to ask them and use the results to sharpen your entire operation.

Give Yourself a Lift

The ideal goal of professional and economic independence can make the necessary work suggested here worth it. Taking action can have a wonderful impact on your morale. It comes from the feeling that you are constantly building.

You can help yourself get early results by establishing a timetable for doing the work. This will give you some satisfying momentum, and that momentum will help to convince you that you are really getting somewhere. Each step you take successfully provides you with the encouragement to take the next one. Try it and see.

A Cheerful Thought

While you are slogging through the early stages of developing your service it can help to remind yourself that you need only *one* solid service idea. It is not self-executing by any means, but as you gather adequate information from which to develop your service, you can expect to experience rising confidence and some excitement that can cheer you on.

CHAPTER 3

Set Up Your Service

This chapter is designed to help you locate and then set up your service to get maximum personal and professional convenience. Look over the territory first and estimate fixed and variable costs in advance. Find ways to establish clear cost control and avoid financial surprises. Examine suggestions aimed at reducing your start-up costs to fit practical needs. There are also sources of outside counsel that can save you time, trouble, and mistakes. They may also help you establish your new service on a solid business basis.

Evaluating a Location

Do you expect your clients or customers to come to you or will you go to them? If you can arrange to visit them, you can reduce your overhead costs by establishing more modest working quarters.

If your clients or customers are going to come to you, there may be need for something more elaborate, which can increase your set-up costs.

Sometimes, appearances are helpful in developing the confidence of clients at a certain level, and this tends to make larger set-up costs necessary. Try to avoid exaggerations on this score or getting "lost" in the decoration of your quarters. An excessively lavish office can work against you with some people. Some prospects take one look and begin to feel that they would be paying for your luxury

... your ego trip. A middle ground is probably best for selling purposes.

One large team got together and spent nearly $300,000 decorating their midtown Manhattan offices before they had a single client, and then they couldn't get one. This is a fact. It illustrates the need to be practical and thoughtful about your choices.

Some Personal Considerations

A lot depends on your kind of service and your temperament. Some people can work happily alone. Others need the stimulation of company. Still others can work at home without driving their families up the walls. Your preferences on these points can influence your choice of location. If possible, it is often best to have one place to work and another to relax. Why? Because when you start on your own there is a strong tendency to work on the development of your service all the time. It helps to make a break in this routine.

A self-sufficient work site with all your working materials and equipment almost within arm's length can save you an amazing amount of wear and tear. Working arrangements that give you freedom to concentrate without interruption are equally important in getting maximum results from your time. Try for short travel time to your work location. A long commute can use up a lot of valuable working time just when you need it most. The ideal goal is maximum working efficiency and convenience in an easy-to-reach location that is large enough to house everything you need.

Some Business Considerations

Can you find a location within your budget that will let you reach your clients or customers easily in all weather with minimum lost time, a location that will give you the kind of acceptance you feel you need considering the level of client or customer you seek or expect? Many clients want to have the services they use convenient to them. It is a selling point of sorts and it is also a useful consideration in selecting a location that will give you maximum results.

Some professional and specialized services need their own kinds of outside help. A location where your kind of suppliers are handy can save you time and help make the performance and delivery of your service more convenient to you. A location near prospective clients or customers can also reduce your selling time and costs.

The real objective is to get maximum dollar value from your location in terms of day-to-day working convenience, easy access to any outside suppliers or services you need, and convenience from your prospective clients' viewpoint. If you can bring all these factors together, you'll have a real winner!

Some Locations to Explore

The most economical place to start is likely to be in your own home. If you can turn a room or a corner of a room into your working quarters you can really keep your start-up costs down and may even have a modest tax advantage. Ask an accountant for the facts in your situation.

Here's another choice: rent desk space in a central business location in your area. Take a look in the telephone book for an outfit that offers this kind of service. This move will give you an immediate place to work, an address, a telephone answering service, and probably some company. You may even find a location that gives you other values. A few phone calls will get you some quick information and costs. As you explore locations, inquire about particular services in different buildings, aiming to fill your needs as you see them.

Here's a third choice: can you move in with a friend in your field? This can work well because there is the possibility of exchanging your services for rent. You do some work for your friend to cut your start-up costs. If you decide to exchange services, do it on a clear time basis. Don't be vague. Agree to give him or her a certain number of hours each month, at a specific hourly rate, in exchange for rent. Keep a record of the time used. This will give you some dignity and avoid a deterioration of the relationship. You will be earning your way and not getting a handout. That can make a lot of difference, and protects the interests of both sides.

Here's a fourth choice: rent a small office of your own in a location that suits you. You may find one through the same outfits that rent desk space. There may be one waiting in a large building that rents small space. Take a look at buildings that are converting apartments to offices. Ask building management staffs or employees about the availability of small space. Look in the newspaper. Ask a local real estate office to point out buildings that have small space available. Be sure to shop around.

Here are some ideas to keep in mind that will help you get

maximum value. Ask if the building is open 24 hours a day, 7 days a week—you may want to work on weekends. Ask if the heat, air conditioning, and other equipment are operating then. Ask what the rent includes: some include electricity, office cleaning, and window cleaning; others do not. Find out precisely what is included. You can expect your rent to be tied to the Consumer Price Index and to go up with that index. Are there other tenants who could become suppliers to you? Are there possible clients? If you like a particular building and there is no space available, ask if one of the tenants has some to sublet. No harm in asking!

Ask yourself this question before you sign the lease: How many working days will it take to pay the annual rent bill? This is a useful evaluation to help keep your rent overhead from turning into undertow later. You may want to check the lease with your lawyer. You can also check on "month-to-month" availability as well as a full year lease or more. See what's available to suit your situation.

Buildings usually rent only space. You have to furnish that space with your own furniture and equipment. Here are two economical places to look for used furniture: (1) check on offices that are closing or moving by asking the managements of buildings; you may be able to get some really good buys; (2) check on close-out auctions. If you don't find what you want, there's always the possibility of renting furniture and some of the standard office equipment, which can help you avoid large outlays at the beginning.

Find the Right Accountant

It is important to consult an accountant during the early stages of setting up your service . . . unless you are one. There are both financial and tax puzzles an accountant can help you to resolve in your special situation. If you have been working in a job and don't happen to have an accountant, you can find one by asking your banker, a lawyer, an insurance broker, or real estate person. They all work closely with accountants.

The "right" accountant is a Certified Public Accountant (not a bookkeeper posing as an accountant) who has a comprehensive background, preferably someone with a range of experience with small business and a variety of clients. An accountant in a small firm who is versatile and interested in "new" or start-up situations could be a good choice for you.

He or she will want to know what your service is and does; the types of expenses you expect to run up; what kinds of clients you are seeking; the basis on which you expect to bill your service; the kind of outside assistance you expect to use; the kinds of materials and equipment you need. You may not have clear answers to all these questions and your accountant will understand. He or she can also help you to identify expenses that are tax deductible. Do the best you can and let your accountant take it from there.

You can tell if you have the right accountant because he or she listens to your questions, gives you clear answers, and is articulate about what he or she is doing. If financial information like this is new to you, it is important to be patient. It will take time to understand fully everything an accountant can tell you. But over a period of time you will begin to feel that your accountant understands your situation and your special needs. Find out the cost of this service by asking. When your needs are clear, you will get a clear answer. It is important to cover this point frankly to make the relationship comfortable for both of you. After some experience you will begin to realize the value of a single accountant who knows you and your special situation. He or she can be of continuing and increasing value as your service grows.

If you are weak with numbers and a bit vague about how to establish your service on a businesslike and profitable basis an accountant can help you. Here are some examples. Your accountant can help you calculate your hourly rate so that it is profitable in your special situation. You can find out how to handle the funds you invest in your service for tax purposes. You can learn how to retain the largest amount of income while paying the least legitimate tax in your special situation. You can find out how to handle social security or develop continuing medical coverage. An accountant will help you set up your books and explain how they work in your situation. These are examples of the contributions an experienced CPA can make to your start-up situation.

Find the Right Lawyer

You can locate a good lawyer by asking your accountant or the same people you checked when you wanted to find your accountant. The lawyer may also be a partner in a small firm interested in start-up situations. Lawyers specialize, and the right one for you is likely to be one who practices general business law (as compared to such specialists as trial lawyers, corporate lawyers, and others). The right lawyer can tell you if there are any laws that apply to your service. He or she can also interpret those laws and help you respond to them appropriately. He or she can tell you if there are any regulations that relate to your situation, and can advise you of any permits, registrations, and other formalities that may be necessary. Tell your lawyer what your service is and does . . . let him or her take it from there. Your lawyer can also tell you whether or not you need to incorporate. A corporation is a shield protecting people inside from personal and, particularly, financial liability beyond the amount invested. Once your situation is known to a lawyer, you will be able to find out whether incorporating would be useful or not. You can also find out the cost of meeting any legal requirements that are part of your situation. Don't hesitate to ask about legal fees. Your lawyer can tell you when your situation and needs are clear. Knowing the cost of professional services (including your own) adds to mutual confidence and helps both sides get the job done.

Anticipate Your Set-up Costs

The charts just ahead can help you define your start-up costs in advance to avoid financial surprises. If you are new to this kind of thing, be patient. You may look all this over and feel a little intimidated—financially. Don't let it throw you. As you will see, some people can get started with a few hundred dollars.

There are three kinds of investment involved: (1) your personal investment to establish your service, (2) an investment in fixed overhead, (3) an investment in variable overhead.

Many of the items mentioned here can be priced by taking a tour of suppliers and available services that reflect your choices. You can always start modestly (most people do) and then add on when you are ready. The purpose here is to define facts so that you can establish firm cost control from the beginning.

There is room on the charts to fill in your own dollar amounts so that you can see them clearly and avoid surprises. In this connection, there is also a 20 percent contingency suggested to cover the guesswork that is an essential part of any estimate.

Your Personal Investment

	ESTIMATE	ACTUAL
Letterheads, envelopes, and business cards	$ _____	$ _____
Your professional equipment	$ _____	$ _____
Your professional information or materials	$ _____	$ _____
Office supplies	$ _____	$ _____
Accounting services	$ _____	$ _____
Legal services	$ _____	$ _____
Total	$ _____	$ _____
Contingency/20%	$ _____	$ _____
Total	$ _____	$ _____

If you work at home, it is quite possible to start your service economically. When you add up the figures on the chart, you may find that you can start for a few hundred dollars. Additional start-up expenses depend on your own choices.

Fixed Expenses

If you work outside your home, renting desk space or furnished office space from a friend in your field, you will have additional start-up costs. Watch out for *permanent* overhead costs like rent, telephone, and secretarial service. Try to keep them to a minimum to avoid early financial pressure and give yourself maximum flexibility and as much start-up time as you can get within your budget.

	ESTIMATE	ACTUAL
Rent	$ _____	$ _____
Telephone service deposit	$ _____	$ _____
Telephone answering service or machine	$ _____	$ _____
Total	$ _____	$ _____
Contingency/20%	$ _____	$ _____
Total	$ _____	$ _____

Before you sign a lease or request telephone installation (requiring a deposit) ask yourself how long it will take you to earn the revenue needed to pay these fixed costs on an annual basis, at your hourly rate. This can help to keep you from creating a situation where your overhead turns into undertow.

Variable Expenses

A lot depends on your budget, service, and viewpoint. These variable expense items are reminders for your review. Toss out items that don't fit and add new ones you want in the space provided. It is possible to estimate some, but others will be a pure guess. Do your best in order to establish as much cost control as possible from the outset. Check with an accountant to see that you get all the tax advantages available in your special situation; many of these items are likely to be tax deductible and/or depreciable for tax purposes.

	ESTIMATE	ACTUAL
New office furniture	$ _____	$ _____
Moving furniture in	$ _____	$ _____
Office decoration	$ _____	$ _____
Secretarial service	$ _____	$ _____
Travel to prospects in other cities	$ _____	$ _____
Entertainment	$ _____	$ _____
Outside suppliers of professional or specialized work	$ _____	$ _____
Resource information or materials needed to perform your service	$ _____	$ _____
Preparation and mailing of announcement letters or other material	$ _____	$ _____
Special facilities such as conference room rental or similar arrangements if needed	$ _____	$ _____
Special equipment rental to perform service, such as projectors, etc.	$ _____	$ _____
Short-term clerical help	$ _____	$ _____

	ESTIMATE	ACTUAL
Office furniture rental	$ _____	$ _____
Office equipment rental	$ _____	$ _____
_____	$ _____	$ _____
_____	$ _____	$ _____
_____	$ _____	$ _____
_____	$ _____	$ _____
_____	$ _____	$ _____
_____	$ _____	$ _____
_____	$ _____	$ _____
_____	$ _____	$ _____
_____	$ _____	$ _____
_____	$ _____	$ _____
_____	$ _____	$ _____
Total	$ _____	$ _____
Contingency/20%	$ _____	$ _____
Total	$ _____	$ _____

A Cheerful Thought

Researching the information to establish clear set-up costs can be a real chore. A careful job can save you unpleasant financial surprises, so it's worth it. The cheerful thought—you have to do it only once.

CHAPTER 4

Price Your Service

Use this chapter to put a dollar price on your service that will cover your overhead, taxes, and a profit. Find out how to handle your price with maximum flexibility, estimate your time, forecast your annual income, and establish good business relationships. Use the guidelines here to help you estimate a vague assignment and define mark-ups. Find out how to discuss your price comfortably, confirm your estimates, bill your work, and collect earned revenue. Recognize situations where continuing fees are practical and adapt standard fee arrangements described here to your special situation. Discover how to recognize a good deal when one shows up and then see how it can keep changing as you prosper.

What Are You Pricing?

The fact that knowledge, experience, and talent don't always mix comfortably with money doesn't tell you anything. When you want to put a price on *your* services it can be like suddenly turning a corner and coming face to face with your own ego. This is a direct route to economic confusion . . . if not oblivion.

What *are* you pricing? You are putting a dollar amount on the time it takes you to get a particular solution to a particular problem that your client or customer is paying you to resolve. It takes knowledge, experience, judgment, and a reasonable length of time to produce reliable results. That *time* is priceable. It can be priced on the basis of both time and value. Both these qualities can be built into your hourly rate.

A Personal Conflict

Many professionals and specialists think in terms of the product of their work. They also wonder what their peers will think of a particular solution. They really want recognition and reassurance that can come only from their peers. Sometimes creative people concentrate almost exclusively on their need to express themselves, their ideas, their opinions, their viewpoints. This is quite natural.

This concentration and many professional measurements of a "job well done" can obscure its monetary value. Some specialists think that the job is done when their *part* of the work is completed. This can lead to exaggerated ideas of the value of the results which, in turn, can produce equally exaggerated ideas of personal earning potentials. These attitudes or approaches can cause considerable economic rejection. In other words, if you charge too much, you won't have any takers. Extremely modest ideas of the value of knowledge based time can be equally unrealistic. Somewhere in the middle is probably the best starting point. In fact, the very idea that *your* time is worth money takes some getting used to when you first move from a salaried job into your own service.

One of the prime purposes of this chapter is to help you establish a profitable hourly rate and then learn to make it work for you. Many professional and specialized services operate on a *time* basis and you can adopt this approach with confidence. It is widely used and broadly accepted in many different marketplaces.

Look Behind Your Salary

When you receive a salary as a member of a team you are using your organization's resources—their office space, equipment, prestige, reputation, and all the other tangible and intangible resources that back up *their* offer of service.

Your "on your own" service does not include the resources of an organization, so that even if you do the same general kind of work, your personal offer of service is different and so is your dollar value. You can run into trouble if you borrow an hourly rate based on what others in your field "say" they charge. What you need is an hourly rate that is profitable to you based on your own offer of service, your own resources, your own overhead, and your special situation.

Let's take a quick look at how salaries are established in service firms generally. Many service firms pay a salary based on competition in the current marketplace. When certain knowledge, experience, or talent is scarce, the salary levels for those individuals go up. Once a person is hired on the basis of those competitive salary levels, the employer then figures out how much business is needed to support the new employee. Then the hourly rate is calculated. Notice the sequence in a salaried situation. Competition sets the level. Then a calculation establishes an hourly rate. Every firm has different overhead figures to work with. Your salary was based in part on the overhead of your company. That's why you can't use your salary as the basis for charging for your time on your own. Only with your own hourly rate, with your own overhead, taxes, and a profit built in, will you know that you are on solid ground. Work out your hourly rate and stick to it. This is where an accountant can really help.

Figure Your Overhead

A basic rule-of-thumb estimate for office expenses, travel, entertainment, stationery, and everything else connected with the overhead of a service business is roughly between 30 and 40 percent of gross annual revenues. This overhead is built into the hourly rate and covered by it.

Here's an example of how it works. Suppose you develop revenue at the rate of $200 a day (about $28.50 an hour) for 200 billable seven-hour days in a year. The gross revenue would be about $40,000. You would have to subtract rent, telephone, and other overhead costs. If they add up to 30 percent of that $40,000, you would have to subtract $12,000 from it, leaving you with a net income of $28,000. You will still have taxes to pay. If they are roughly 25 percent (each situation is different), then the $28,000 will be reduced by $7,000. This leaves you with a net spendable income of $21,000 after overhead and taxes are paid.

You can also start planning with your personal income goals or needs. Suppose you decide that you want a net income of $30,000 annually. Multiply that amount by one and two-thirds. This produces the amount of $50,000. Divide that amount by 200 billable days and you get a daily rate of $250. Then subtract for overhead and taxes and find out what your net spendable income will be.

To arrive at an hourly billing rate, it is important to consider what your needs are and whether or not your offer of service is worth your billing rate to your prospective clients or customers. This throws a sharp focus on the quality and excellence of your service—an essential factor in its basic value. A critical element is the sale of those 200 billable days each year.

Why Plan on 200 Billable Days?

If you sell your service on a standard "time" basis, here's what you are working with. Like everyone else, you start with 365 days a year. Take away 104 days for weekends and you have 261 working days left. Take away those 12 national holidays that produce three-day weekends and you have 249 working days left. Take away a standard 2-week vacation and you have 235 working days left. Take away 35 of *those* working days for inside administration, selling, accounting, and other unbillable activity and you have a maximum of 200 billable days available each year. You can work more or less, of course. But the 200 days offer a planning base for estimating annual income using 7-hour days multiplied by your selected hourly rate. It will take time to "fill up" those 200 billable days but they offer a reasonable goal.

For selling purposes, you can work both time and value into your hourly rate. For instance, you can charge less for time when the work is routine and your client sees tangible and usable results. You can charge more per hour for value when the work takes special knowledge, experience, talent, or judgment and your client gets satisfactory results.

Seven Ways People Get Paid

The method you use should be simple, clear, and understandable to you and your clients. It should be "standard" in your field so that your prospects will accept it and you. Operating on a time basis with an hourly rate fills many of these needs. Here are seven ways people get paid; see if there is something else here that you can use.

1. By the hour
2. By the day
3. By the job
4. By a standard commission
5. By cost plus a percentage
6. By fees based on time
7. By fees plus time or royalties

The real problem is to relate your time and what it accomplishes for *you* in income and satisfaction to what it produces for your *client* in results, satisfaction, or revenue.

You are on solid ground when you decide to base your hourly rates and billing on sound practices and learn to make those practices produce income for you. You are also wise to set an hourly rate and use it on all assignments until you have a track record and feel comfortable handling your rate.

Here is an hours-to-dollars chart that can help you forecast annual revenues. A 30 percent overhead is reflected in the chart. You may be able to beat the overhead percentage at the beginning. It is only a guideline. Put in your own overhead rate to get a clear picture in your special situation.

Hours-to-Dollars Scale

HOURLY RATE	INCOME FROM 200 7-HOUR DAYS	LESS 30% FOR OVER-HEAD	WHAT YOU HAVE TO SPEND BEFORE TAXES
$ 15.00	$ 21,000	$ 6,300	$14,700
$ 17.50	$ 24,500	$ 7,930	$17,150
$ 20.00	$ 28,000	$ 8,400	$19,600
$ 22.50	$ 31,500	$ 9,450	$22,050
$ 25.00	$ 35,000	$10,500	$24,500
$ 27.50	$ 38,500	$11,550	$26,950
$ 30.00	$ 42,000	$12,600	$29,400
$ 35.00	$ 49,000	$14,700	$34,300
$ 40.00	$ 56,000	$16,800	$39,200
$ 45.00	$ 63,000	$18,900	$44,100
$ 50.00	$ 70,000	$21,000	$49,000
$ 55.00	$ 77,000	$23,100	$53,900
$ 60.00	$ 84,000	$25,200	$58,800
$ 65.00	$ 91,000	$27,300	$63,700
$ 70.00	$ 98,000	$29,400	$68,600
$ 75.00	$105,000	$31,500	$73,500
$ 80.00	$112,000	$33,600	$78,400
$ 85.00	$119,000	$35,700	$83,300
$ 90.00	$126,000	$37,800	$88,200
$ 95.00	$133,000	$39,900	$93,100
$100.00	$140,000	$42,000	$98,000

Look Inside Your Hourly Rate

It is important to be *sure* that your hourly rate will cover your personal needs. If it won't earn you a reasonable living, you won't be happy doing the work and you won't be able to do a good job. It is your hourly rate combined with your ability to do effective work that is the real essence of financial security when you are on your own.

Your hourly rate must cover your personal needs, your overhead, your taxes, and still produce a profit for future growth. It is important to be sure *beforehand* that your rate *will* do these jobs for you. Here are some basic percentages you can apply to help you find out.

30% for overhead
25% for taxes—or as your personal situation indicates
45% for real income—or as your personal situation indicates.

The 45% can be treated as salary and profit.

You will have to adjust these percentages to reflect your personal overhead and tax situations. You can give yourself a sense of security by paying yourself a salary and by deliberately putting the profit aside for future growth. You can also prepare for "tax time" by putting the tax percentage into a savings account *each time* you receive funds. Then you will be developing "interest income" from it as well as gaining some peace of mind regarding your taxes.

Give Yourself Flexibility

The right hourly rate for your kind of work can help you in many different ways. For instance, it can help you define your market. The higher your hourly rate compared with that of your competitors, the fewer real prospects you are likely to find. The lower your hourly rate competitively, the more prospects you are likely to find. It's probably best to start somewhere in the middle until you learn how to work with your hourly rate. It takes time.

Your hourly rate lets you estimate assignments. It helps you compete when you really want an assignment by reducing the rate slightly. It helps you keep your service practical and competitive. Your profit is built in so that you know that most assignments will be profitable automatically.

An hourly rate can be easily translated into a daily rate on the basis of the standard 7-hour day. You can develop a background for estimating by recording the time it takes you to complete different kinds of assignments as you go along. You can account for special situations by adding a bit more to your hourly rate for overtime, weekend work, special rush jobs, and the like. This means a "bit more" for those extra hours only.

Remember, the real problem is to relate your time to what it accomplishes for you *and* your clients. This is hard to see and do at first—particularly when there are economic pressures. But when you get this relationship crystal clear you can use your hourly rate with flexibility and selectivity. You can adapt to almost any situation with a sure sense of control.

A Special Opportunity

You may have noticed that large service organizations in your field pay their professionals and specialists both salaries and benefits. For instance, suppose a specialist in a large service firm doing your kind of work earns $28,000 a year, or $20 an hour. The firm also has to pay overhead, insurance, benefits, and other costs. Those costs are covered by charging the specialist's time out to clients at two or three times the $20 he or she is paid. This might mean $40 or $60 an hour that the client will pay.

On some assignments you may be able to do the same work for less than that and still make a profit. The point is that you can *compete* directly with giant firms in your field on some assignments (those that are logical for one person to handle) and have the advantage because you can make a profit charging less than the large firm *must* charge. At the same time, your client will get your full attention, a job well done, and still make a saving. This is an opportunity you might want to explore. Don't hesitate to go after "big fish" because you *can* compete in this interesting marketplace.

Estimating Your Time

If you are planning to do much the same kind of work on your own as you do in your present job, you can get a head start toward estimating your time by accurately timing the kind of assignments you expect to get. Count all your time. Research. Meetings. The actual work, including false starts. Time everything from the start of the work to a point where you have your first visable and usable results . . . and keep going right through to the completed job. Over a period of time you can establish factual "time norms" for certain recurring assignments that can be invaluable for estimating purposes later on.

Even though assignments may differ in content, the time and *means* of arriving at solutions are often the same in a given area of specialization. It is also important to give consideration to the level of quality that is wanted. Some assignments deserve less time by their very nature. Others are more important and deserve an all-out effort. Select assignments in a range so that you can establish your own "time norms" that will give you a solid basis for estimating when you establish your own service.

Remember, when you take on a new assignment for a new client, you usually can't afford to charge for *all* the time you have to put in. You have new things to learn and that "learning process" should be on your own time.

Forecast Your Income

You can save a lot of anxiety by planning on an annual basis. Then you can see more clearly what you are working with and it becomes easier to establish specific annual revenue goals. The purpose, among other things, is to avoid facing a "do-or-die" situation where you *must* get a particular assignment because you need the money. This can throw off your judgment. It pays to consider candidly your special abilities, skills, interests, and experience and what they can produce for your clients or customers. The graph titled "When Your Time Is Money" is a financial planning tool that visualizes the interrelationship between your time and income at different hourly rates. For instance, at $35 an hour it would take 1,000 hours to produce an annual gross income of $35,000. Compare this with the fact that most people in salaried jobs work about 1,600 hours a year. When you are on your own, it boils down to the number of billable hours or days you can sell in one year.

The graph also shows an increase in overhead as you develop more activity. This reflects the increased cost of selling your service.

FIXED EXPENSES. These are standard items like rent, telephone, telephone answering service, and other continuing overhead costs that remain the same. They are tax deductible when properly recorded.

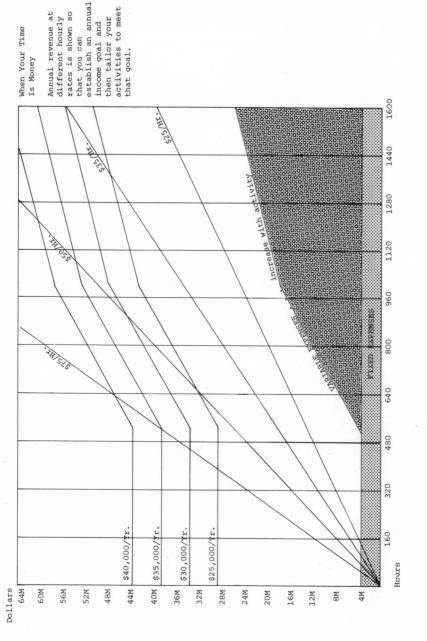

When Your Time
Is Money

Annual revenue at
different hourly
rates is shown so
that you can
establish an annual
income goal and
then tailor your
activities to meet
that goal.

VARIABLE EXPENSES. Here, the emphasis is on selling costs and they are deliberately on the high side. In fact, they may be fattening as well since most of them involve entertainment. This comes up when someone wants to know about your service and you take them to lunch or dinner. Here are some specific assumptions about these selling costs. For 540 to 1,000 billable hours the selling cost is $0 to $14 for each billable hour; this represents 6 lunches or dinners per week at $50 each . . . at 1,000 hours for 48 weeks.

For 1,000 to 1,600 billable hours the cost of selling is $14 per billable hour. This represents 9 lunches or dinners per week at $50 each . . . at 1,500 hours for 50 weeks. The more activity of this kind, the greater your selling costs. This accounts for the projected increase.

These selling costs are tax deductible when properly recorded. It is important to take into account your estimate of the need for entertainment and the cost of selling your service as part of your financial planning.

Establish Good Business Relationships

Many professional and specialized services work on the basis of specific assignments or projects. Many of these projects are vague at the beginning. That's why it is important to establish simple procedures that can make both the assignment and the business relationship clear to each side.

Sound procedures can make the difference between a single assignment and a continuing relationship. They may also make the difference between getting paid and not getting paid. Many professional and specialized services are "perishable" in the sense that once the work is done it can't be taken back again.

Here are several steps that can help you establish good professional and business relationships during the discussion of a new assignment or project.

THE FIRST STEP. Start with an agreement on what your client wants: his specific goal, purpose, objective, or definition of the assignment from his viewpoint. This means that *you* have a specific job to do which is a step toward *his* ultimate goal.

After discussion, write his purpose down in a *brief defining sentence* and ask him to review, edit, or approve it so that you feel sure that you both understand it to mean the *same* thing.

For an architect starting a new project, this sentence might read: "We want to develop a preliminary plan for the layout of an addition to the existing building to house the facilities of the research department. Is that right?" For a public relations man, this sentence might read: "We want to develop a series of appearances before Chambers of Commerce in New York, Chicago, Dallas, and San Francisco. Is that right?" For an engineer, this sentence might read: "We want to find a new way to reduce friction in the drive mechanism to cut down on wear. Is that right?" For an advertising man, this sentence might read: "We want to develop a series of messages aimed at your dealers to stimulate their participation in the new service program we are offering all customers. Is that right?"

This defining sentence can do several jobs for you. It is *your* starting point for doing the work. It is also your introduction when you present the work later on. This repetition reminds your client and gives your work quick perspective and relevance again. Remember, he or she may have had a lot of other things go on since you started to work on the assignment. Just before introducing the work, the advertising man might say: "Remember, we wanted to develop a series of messages to stimulate dealer participation in our new service program. Here are our suggestions." This opening remark gives the client a way to measure the solution that is partially objective. This simple "defining sentence" device for making a vague assignment clear can eliminate a lot of misunderstanding and fault-finding that can wreck a carefully built relationship.

THE SECOND STEP. Make the financial details clear. Do this before you invest too much of your own time or money. Make clear what you will do, what it will cost the client, when he or she will get results, when and how payment is due. Your client needs to know this in order to buy your service comfortably.

A THIRD STEP. Send the client a confirmation letter that outlines your understanding of the work you will perform and includes the financial details . . . before you become too involved. Your client's initials on this letter gives you a solid position from which to collect later on.

If you are working with a brand-new client, here are some other steps that can protect the relationship, particularly if large sums are involved.

ASK THE CLIENT FOR A BANK REFERENCE. If you get an exaggerated expression of "insult" from your client he is likely to be either broke and on the defensive or doing so well he really is insulted. Take your pick. But remember, nobody has ever seen a poorly dressed confidence man. So don't rely on appearances, big names, or word of mouth.

This is what the bank will tell you. "The balance is in the low three figures," which means about $250. "Moderate three figures," means $350 to $450. "High three figures" means around $900. These are modest figures, of course. But they illustrate the pattern you can expect.

ASK THE CLIENT'S SUPPLIERS. Call the accounting departments of suppliers and discreetly inquire about their "experience" with payment from your new client. They may say "slow 60," which means they get paid in 60 days but it's slow. This will give you an idea of what to expect.

Almost everyone agrees with this thought: if you have a strong negative feeling when your client discusses estimates and budgets, *trust it.* Then move only one step at a time and don't invest too much of your own time or money without payment of some kind. This could be a good time to use progressive billing shaped to fit the situation. More about that later.

Estimating a Vague Assignment

This is where that brief defining sentence can help you again. It's the starting point for your estimate. Most vague assignments have natural stopping points. For instance, an architectural project might start with some research and then the development of preliminary drawings to produce the *first* rough idea of the direction a particular project should take. Then, on approval, the next steps would take place until the project was completed.

Estimate the time it would take you to reach the first natural stopping point in your kind of work on a specific assignment. Make it the first point where you can show visible results. Use your hourly rate to turn this time estimate into dollars. You may want to use a "minimum-to-maximum" approach, which is a standard practice. It will help you cover the inevitable "gray areas" that form part of any project.

Then estimate a rough budget for your work on the total assignment as you understand it. Again, it can help to use the minimum-to-maximum approach, which protects you and helps your client to avoid unpleasant surprises. Your client needs to know the cost of the first step and the total estimated budget for your service through to the completion of your work on the assignment.

You can reassure him or her by frankly stating that your estimate for the total budget is on the "high" side for safety's sake. You will, of course, charge only for the time actually used.

It boils down to working on a vague assignment until you have crystallized it to a point where budgeting and estimating are going to be reliable. By then, it is no longer a vague assignment. When you have your estimate completed, put it to this practical test. Ask yourself: "What is the objective value of the results I will produce?" You may want to modify or adjust your estimate as a result of your answer to that question. But you can be sure that it is the first thought that will arise when your client sees your estimate. Try and get there first and work toward sound financial relationships.

Estimating for a Team

Suppose you develop an assignment where there is a need for a temporary team of related talents from your field, a situation where each member of your temporary team wants to stay independent. Everyone who works with you on such an assignment should work as he or she wants to work. Some may prefer straight time turned into dollar amounts. Others may want to give you a minimum-to-maximum estimate. Still others may want to estimate a flat amount if the work is clear enough. What counts is their total dollar estimates for their *parts* of the work. The problem is to relate their work to what it will produce in terms of results toward the completion of your assignment. Your client is paying for those results.

The first step is a thorough discussion of the assignment to develop a really clear definition of what it is and what each member is to do. Then each team member can provide a dollar estimate of the amount needed to get visible results on his or her part of the work. Here is what an estimate by two people working with you on a project might consist of:

George Smith	5 days	$40 hr/$280 a day	$1,400
Stan Jones	3–4 days	$30 hr/$210 a day	$630–$840
Total including Stan Jones's maximum estimate for his work			$2,240

The purpose is to establish a clear, fair, and complete understanding so that *all* members of your team retain their independence and receive financial returns according to their contribution to results on your assignment. It is equally important to establish a sound financial approach that is satisfying to each member so that effective performance can be followed by immediate payment when the assignment is completed or when your client pays your bill.

Define Your Markups

The fairest way to determine your markup is to make certain that all members of your team are paid for the amount of time and involvement they put into your assignment. It is *your* assignment, however, and you need to be compensated for your supervisory time and the responsibility you take for results to your client. You can mark up the hourly rate that George and Stan give you. For instance, if you are paying George $40 an hour, you may want to mark that up to $50 an hour or more to cover your supervisory time. Or you may take their total bills and add a markup of 20 or 30 percent to cover your time and responsibility. There are often "standard" markups in different professions and specialties and you should know what the practice is in your area in order to stay competitive.

Each situation is different. These markup procedures need to be modified to the practicalities of your situation. For instance, consider the objective value of the work to your client. It can come down to this: fairness to your client; fairness to your temporary team members; fairness to you. A reasonable markup that produces a fair profit can make the difference between a continuing and profitable relationship with your client and an expensive "one-shot" where you are left looking for a new client.

Some professions and specialities have materials or mechanical steps that are also marked up. There are usually standard approaches to this kind of markup and you should know what they are if they are part of your situation. In advertising, for example, the material or mechanical side would cover such items as typesetting, photography, art work, and similar needs.

Discussing Your Estimate

It is important to demonstrate that you are sincerely thinking, talking, and acting in your client's best interests. You must believe that your estimate or fee is fair to your client or you won't be able to convince him or her.

People who discuss prices all the time believe that most reasonable prospects will accept the most expensive services when they are convinced that they will get *their idea* of value. The real job is to convince your prospect of the value of your service in direct relationship to what he or she wants to accomplish. Show how your service or solution will help to achieve the desired objectives.

Here are some points and thoughts you can adapt to your situation when it comes to discussing your estimate.

Connect the results of your service or your specific solution to the accomplishment of your client's short- or long-term objectives.

Concentrate on how your service will satisfy a client's reason for buying it in the first place—his or her basic motivation.

Demonstrate the quality of your service by briefly defining the steps you will take to complete the work.

If available, you can bring out the special, exclusive, or one-of-a-kind qualities in your background which will give your prospect a clear advantage or benefit.

If true, suggest that the results of your service can be shared by other people in your client's organization thus increasing its evident value.

If true, you can demonstrate that the results of your service will save your client time, money, or develop additional or new revenue.

If true, you can suggest that your service will save the time of important people in your client's organization or help to make better use of their available resources.

If true, suggest that your handling of the assignment will relieve the client of personal responsibility in a touchy political situation.

If true, suggest that your service tends to pay for itself with the first use and that your client will continue to receive benefits long afterward.

Try to avoid stating your hourly rate in abstract because it can cause misunderstanding. Unsophisticated (about your field) but good prospects can hear "$60 an hour" subjectively and think that you are earning far more than they are. They may not realize that you don't earn that amount every single day of the year. They might also make a quick judgment that tells them that you are "too expensive" when the value you can offer is just what they are looking for. It is often better to simply state your estimate in direct relationship to the project. Keep things simple, clear, and to the point. Give a single amount or a minimum-to-maximum estimate and make it as clear as you can to avoid misunderstanding later on.

Confirm Your Estimate

A confirmation letter helps your client because it confirms that you are working on a specific problem or portion of his needs that he wants you to work on. It helps you because it clearly establishes that you are doing the work in the event that such clarification is needed later on. Your confirmation letter also allows you gracefully to reopen the point about payment before you put in too much time.

A confirmation letter can include a clear statement of what you are going to do . . . the amount and method of payment . . . any special expenses . . . what your client will contribute to the work . . . and anything that is obviously left out of the project that may be handled by someone else. Here is an example:

> Dear _____
>
> This will confirm our understanding of the assignment we discussed yesterday. We will plan, research, and prepare a brochure about your services through to fininished text and layout in two colors.
>
> We expect this will be completed in about 10 days. Our estimate for this work is between $3,000 and $3,500.
>
> We understand that you will provide all necessary photographs and specific information about individuals who will appear in the material. We also understand that we are responsible for preparation up to but not including printing.
>
> We are going ahead on this basis now. If you would like to make any adjustments, please give me a call. Please initial and return the attached copy at your convenience.
>
> Sincerely,

If the client does *not* return the copy in a reasonable length of time and before you have invested too much time or money in the work, you have a reasonable pretext for asking for clarification of the situation without straining the relationship.

Bill Your Assignment

Your bill should explain "what was done" as related to "what was wanted" in the first place. It is here that you may be able to quote that "brief defining sentence" you formulated at the start of your assignment. The more you use your client's actual words in your bill, the more likely he or she is to remember, understand, and accept it.

If your client receives your bill and knows that the service has been performed properly, there should be no problem. If you have encountered problems or bill something outside the original estimate, this addition should be made clear in your bill. Then your client knows *why* there is a difference between the original estimate and the bill you have sent in.

Since many services are "perishable" and soon forgotten, many professionals and specialists render their bills *with* the completed assignment or soon thereafter. If you delay too long, your client may forget what you did and resist your bill accordingly.

Your bill may also contain a clear statement of your out-of-pocket expenses. The inclusion of these expenses should be agreed upon in advance so that there are no surprises for your client. You can list these expenses under the word "disbursements" on your bill. You can get very detailed but it isn't usually worth it. However, it is a good idea to judge the "appropriateness" of billing some out-of-pocket items. Sometimes, they should be part of your own overhead because they would represent an annoying nuisance to your client.

It is important to keep up to date with your billing and *keep all aspects open* for review. Otherwise, you are bound to run into difficulties responding to inquiries. Most service bills are backed up by time sheets, bills for out-of-pocket expenses, and other factual evidence. Let your client know that this "evidence" is available and you will increase his or her confidence in you and the integrity of your billing procedures.

Bill as You Go

Another standard method of billing services is called *progressive billing* and it is widely used because it is clear and fair to both sides. With progressive billing, you bill your work as you reach agreed-upon and natural "stopping points" where your client gets visible results. It is fair to your client because he or she has those usable results. It is fair to you because you have performed and delivered satisfactory work. That's why it works.

The actual "billing points" should be logical to your work. With the preparation of a brochure, for instance, the first natural stopping point could be the completion of the necessary research and preparation of a satisfactory text. A second natural stopping point could be the delivery of the completed text with layout. A third natural stopping point would be the delivery of the material ready for printing. Progressive billing is appropriate when your client receives visible and satisfactory results that have a direct relationship on what he or she wanted in the first place.

Payment in Advance

When you are on your own and not in a position to finance elaborate projects, you can *adapt* progressive billing to enable you to participate on a more comfortable financial basis.

In this situation, your client pays one-third of the total estimate in advance. This gives you some "working capital" so that you can afford to start the work. Then, at an agreed-upon and natural stopping point in the work (where your client has visible results) you receive another third of the estimate. The final third, which may include out-of-pocket expenses or any other unexpected items that showed up during the work, is billed and paid on completion of the work.

This approach lets you participate in larger projects than you can finance on your own. It also opens up the use of your services and other qualified resources from your client's viewpoint. This approach is widely used and accepted because it serves both sides.

Collecting Your Fee

If necessary, your original "brief defining sentence" about what your client wanted in the first place and your confirmation letter (whether it was signed or not) can help you in collecting your fees from a client who, for some reason, doesn't want to pay you.

It is important to establish a simple rule: Get the facts about the entire transaction clear before you attempt to settle. Who did what and when? It pays to delay any detailed discussion about a specific settlement until you are in possession of the facts. Then you can save a lot of your own time and temper (as well as those of your client) by using your combined good judgment to arrive at the fairest settlement.

This initial approach aims at helping save the relationship. Your client may be going through problems that you are unaware of and which could easily explain delays in payment. It doesn't help to fly off the handle.

It is important to remember the recommendations of professional credit managers. They insist on making the financial details clear at the outset. You can do the same thing and *avoid* difficult collection problems.

The real issue in avoiding collection problems is simply to make crystal clear in advance what you will do . . . what it will cost . . . when payment is due . . . and when the results of your service will be delivered. The statement of these details in your confirmation letter can help you collect your money.

The purpose of a settlement is to establish a plan for payment over a period of time. It helps if you can arrange this yourself and maintain the relationship. If you *have* to turn to outside sources to collect funds, you will *always* lose. Here are some preliminary questions a lawyer might ask you: (1) What was your agreement? (2) Was there any correspondence covering the situation? (3) Did the client ever tell you to "stop" or that he or she was dissatisfied? (4) Have you ever received a check that was not good? (5) Did he or she ever send you anything after you submitted your bill to indicate that there was an objection? This gives you an idea of the kind of information needed when you use an outside source to collect for you.

The only real protection you have is to make sure to work with the many people and organizations of demonstrated integrity. There is financial security in being *selective* about those you choose to accept as clients. It doesn't cost you anything to make this kind of choice beforehand and it can pay off handsomely.

Establishing Continuing Fees

Sometimes, continuing fee arrangements can go a long way toward resolving financial worry and anxiety when you are on your own.

The principal idea to remember about fees is this: *all fees are based on time.* When you establish a fee you are really estimating the time needed to get a specific job or jobs done. The same basic procedures for estimating a single assignment can be used to establish specific fees. You are making *part* of your time available on a regular basis to get specific jobs done. Your client is buying part of your time on a regular basis to get *those* specific jobs done. There exists in your client's situation a need for continuity of effort and results that offers benefits to both sides.

A lot depends on how precisely the scope of the work is defined in advance. It is helpful to discuss this point at a fundamental level and free of technical talk. It is important to define the projects and get a clear understanding of what your client wants. Then you can estimate the time you need to produce results on those specific projects.

When to Suggest Fees

Here are seven different situations when a continuing fee arrangement may be productive for you and your client.

1. When your client needs your kind of service and wants to avoid establishing an "in-house" capacity which would produce continuing salary and other overhead costs which he or she wants to avoid.

2. When your client has a range of continuing and *predictable* assignments, projects, programs, or needs in your area which keep recurring and he or she wants them "covered" by someone with your special knowledge and experience.

3. When your client has a series of assignments involving special political or personal sensitivity and recognizes that they would be better handled by a qualified outsider who can take responsibility and give the work necessary objectivity.

4. When your client has assignments that require special knowledge, experience, or concentration and doesn't have the qualified people on staff or prefers not to tie up staff members because of other work.

5. When there is too much work to be done and your client doesn't have enough staff people to do it and prefers not to add permanent overhead by hiring new people.

6. When there is a series of assignments with specific deadlines and other pressures and demands and your client needs results not available from his or her staff people.

7. When there is a series of assignments which your client wants to control personally and keep confidential until the work is completed.

Take a hard look at your client's situation to determine if there is a possibility for the acceptance of a continuing fee. It will begin from your client's situation and needs.

Three Continuing Fee Arrangements

Sound fee arrangements provide for the time needed to get the job done, support of that work including necessary materials, supplies, travel, and any other out-of-pocket expenses that are predictable, a sound and fair profit for you, and a clear statement of the time and method of payment. Here are three specific fee arrangements that you may be able to use or adapt to your special situation.

TIME ALONE IS A FEE ARRANGEMENT. Here you commit *part* of your time to your client on a regular basis. Suppose, for example, you guarantee your client five working days a month at $250 a day. You receive the $1,250 and your client receives your five days a month to use against current needs. Your client uses your time to be sure your "area" is covered. However, he or she may not know in advance your specific assignments, because the needs keep changing. It is important to be careful in arrangements like this. It is vital to define the specifics as clearly as possible at the outset. Then you may have to define them again after the first month's experience. The clearer it is in terms of what you are to do, the better.

A FLAT RETAINER. This means that you get a certain amount on a monthly or annual basis. It is practical when there is a clear definition of what it covers. You can break those assignments down and estimate each one to get a total for the retainer. You can use your hourly rate to develop dollar amounts. Make sure you include any out-of-pocket expenses, overhead, travel, materials, and other items that are predictable and relevant to doing the work.

A RETAINER PLUS TIME. This arrangement works well in some situations. The retainer covers the predictable parts of the work. The "time" covers the unpredictable needs that arise in the course of time. This helps both sides. The client has his or her basic needs satisfied but knows that he or she is responsible for meeting unpredictable needs as well. You have a clear amount of revenue that you can rely on and the opportunity of earning more. The time part of this arrangement is based on your standard hourly rate and billed according to the time used in a given month or as agreed.

Two Special Arrangements

REVENUE FOR RESULTS. This is sometimes called "a piece of the action." With this arrangement you provide your service on the basis of your costs plus a fixed percentage of the dollar return your client receives in *additional* or new revenue as a direct result of your work. If there is no additional dollar result to your client, you haven't made anything extra but you have received your costs. If your service does produce additional revenue for your client, you receive a share as your profit. These results are earned, so it is fair to both sides. Your client gets additional or new revenue. You get a share of that addition as your profit. The arrangement should be put in writing to make it clear before the work begins. In some situations you may want to have your accountant and your client's accountant get together to work out the details. This way, you can avoid a direct involvement that might destroy your mystique or change your relationship with your client. You can also avoid a difficult discussion which might damage an otherwise sound relationship. If your client won't agree to an audit of the dollar results, you can make your own judgment about the validity of this approach in that situation.

COST PLUS. In this situation, you complete your service for your costs plus a percentage of those costs, which becomes your profit. For example, your fee for your service might be $1,000, which covers your time, overhead, out-of-pocket expenses, and other costs directly related to delivering your service. Then you add 20 percent (or as agreed) to that $1,000, which becomes your profit. It is important to review anticipated costs beforehand so that they are clear and satisfactory and contain no surprises. You may want to put this understanding in writing to avoid problems later on.

When Their Budget Is Too Small for You

Sometimes you may find that a budget has already been set for your part of an assignment. These budgets are sometimes established by people who don't know the cost of the work and underestimate the needs for budgeting purposes.

Suppose your work on a project has been budgeted for $1,000. When you know what the assignment consists of, you may recognize that you can't produce sound results for the $1,000 at your hourly rate. If this is the case, you are wise to reject the assignment.

There are bound to be many considerations—the caliber of the client, your own financial needs short-term, your other commitments. But if the suggested budget is grossly unrealistic, then you are almost bound to lose in the long run.

It pays to bring this situation to your client's attention frankly. Many reasonable people are quite willing to adjust their budgets for adequate reasons. They want value for their money. They know that excessively modest budgeting can also produce excessively poor results.

Give your client a solid and convincing reason for increasing

CHAPTER 5

Sell Your Service

The information in this chapter can help you establish a selling program that you can operate in minimum time once it is set up. You can start out with an organized approach and test it until you are satisfied. There is room to write in your own ideas so that you can begin to collect your key selling information conveniently in one place—right here—and build solidly one step at a time. You can get ready by building a sound prospect list. You can get really set by reviewing the proven selling tools described here. There is an organized approach to building a convincing sales presentation. You will see ways to open and then walk through new doors comfortably. The purpose is solid control of the sale of your service.

Convince Yourself First

It is important to make the sale of your service interesting to *you*. For instance, try to convince yourself that the work and effort it takes to develop a practical selling program *will* produce the clients, assignments, or revenue you want. This makes the work worthwhile. One critical purpose is to escape from this problem: a situation where you are busy working on assignments until they are completed only to find that you have run out of work. One result can be an undignified dash into the marketplace under pressure to get more projects to pay the rent. This not only is self-defeating but involves the kind of pressure that almost never makes a good bargain.

It is important to avoid this do-or-die struggle and know that there are more fish in the sea, because you have their names. Then you know that you are in a strong position.

This knowledge can give you a valuable sense of confidence when you tackle the actual selling job. You can see that job more objectively and perhaps as both a stimulating challenge and an interesting experience.

The purpose here is to organize and develop a continuing selling program from the beginning—one that puts you in full control and that you can operate in minimum time once it is set up.

Don't be afraid to make mistakes. They'll love you for it. After all, most of us would much rather work with people like ourselves who make mistakes now and then. Do the best planning and selling job you can and build experience steadily until *you* are in full control and *at ease*. The objective is simply to be comfortable in the role of selling your service.

As you read along you will see brief "open" spaces where you can write in your first spontaneous ideas. They are often the best and most reliable.

Are You Prejudiced against Selling?

This is not the farfetched question it may seem to be. For instance, some professionals and specialists would like to stay safely isolated on their mountaintops and have prospective clients come to them almost with hat in hand. It could become quite lonely up there. Many who hold this viewpoint may be reacting to exaggerated ideas about selling. They may look at the art and act of selling as beneath their dignity. They may equate selling with all the cheapness and insincerity of the old-fashioned slap-on-the-back extrovert personality. All that went out of style years ago.

Really effective salesmen are experts who know what they are talking about and can command the respect and confidence that such knowledge deserves. They are sincere, straightforward, and magnificent listeners. They are natural and they stay in character. You may find that you can do the same thing. Look for your kind of people. People with whom the personal chemistry clicks and everything works. They are the people who can become your most prized clients, but you have to find them.

If you have prejudices about the idea of selling, this would be a good time to examine them to see if they really hold up. At the very least, try to avoid having that prejudice work against you when you want to sell your service.

The Natural Steps

A good approach to establishing a selling program when you are starting out is to follow the natural steps that build up to give you control of the sale of your service. Here are the highlights:

A clear definition of your prospective clients so that you are aiming at people who are most likely to accept your service.

The development of evidence that will back up what you say about your service and make it believable and credible.

The preparation of an organized sales presentation which draws on your special evidence for the raw material which forms the basic content.

The translation of your special evidence into advantages, benefits, values, or satisfactions which aim at stimulating your prospect to take action—buy your service.

Practical and proven techniques for opening doors to new prospects.

Effective ways to walk through those doors easily and comfortably.

Next, ways to evaluate each prospect to determine whether there is enough interest to warrant following up.

Finally, the content of a follow-up program that will help your prospect to remember *you* when he or she is ready to buy.

Define Your Job

You can make genuine progress when you give the selling job some specific definition. For instance, here are five steps that never fail to produce results when they are executed carefully and with continuity.

DEVELOP YOUR PROSPECT LIST. You need a list of genuine prospects that is large enough so that *you* have solid belief that you will produce results from it. Define your prospects by name, title, organization, address, telephone number. Call and *make sure* that you will be talking to the right person and that he or she is still there.

PICK YOUR REFERRALS. Clearly identify sources of referral into your marketplace, preferably people who have confidence in you and who enjoy the confidence of the people you want to reach in your marketplace. A good referral depends on the right person asking the right person.

MAKE CONVINCING SALES CALLS. The fact is that few professional and specialized services are accepted on the first call. A first call often seeks to establish your prospect's trust and find out (with him or her) where and how your service fits the needs at the time . . . or in the future.

PUT NUMBERS ON YOUR SIDE. The means of making enough calls on new prospects so that the numbers are always working for you. This gives you a natural build-up of opportunity and a better chance of having the "timing" work out favorably. Then you may almost always have someone who is ready to buy or nearly ready.

MAKE THEM REMEMBER YOU. They will buy your service only when they have the need and are ready to buy. That decision will probably come when you are not there. That's why it is important to make certain that they remember you favorably when they make the decision. You can maintain their awareness with interesting and brief telephone calls, by sending them useful information in the mail, and with short social visits. Concentrate exclusively on prospects who have demonstrated some interest. For instance, use short social visits to help you find out more about an interested prospect's situation or needs—where and how your service might fit and be most useful. There is a special need for thoughtful, interesting, and convincing follow-up.

Define Your Marketplace

A preliminary definition of your marketplace gives you a target for subsequent selling steps. It will help you determine in advance those specific targets where you have the best chance of being accepted. Careful definition of your prospects can help you make the best use of limited selling time and may reduce your cost of selling, too. Consider the following situations:

THE SITUATION WHERE YOU UNDERSTAND THEIR BUSINESS. This has a strong and immediate impact on your credibility to them and gives them useful confidence when it comes to accepting your service. The fact is that most people think that their business is different and unique—whether it is or not. What is different and unique is their way of doing it. In any case, some prospects don't want to "educate" an outsider to their activities. You can save a lot of time by identifying prospects like this as clearly as possible beforehand.

THE SITUATION WHERE THEY USE OUTSIDE SERVICES. Your chances of acceptance go up with prospects who hire and use outside services as a regular part of their operation. The only way to find out is to ask or send a sales letter and find out from the response to it.

THE SITUATION WHERE THEY NEED YOU. Your chances of acceptance go up with prospects who don't have your kind of background and service on staff because they don't need it often enough. But when they do need it, they really need it. Examples: smaller companies, privately held companies, smaller divisions of large corporations who want to do things their way with their own outside help.

THE SITUATION WHERE THEY UNDERSTAND YOUR KIND OF SERVICE. This understanding can save you the long and expensive job of educating a prospect, which can substantially delay your acceptance.

THE SITUATION WHERE THEY CAN AFFORD YOU. The level of your rate or fee helps to define your market. For instance, the higher your fee (competitively) the fewer real prospects you may find. The lower your fee (competitively) the more real prospects you may find. You control it.

THE SITUATION WHERE THEY CAN PAY YOU. Your evaluation of their credit standing and ability to pay your rates or fees can help you develop a sound and profitable operation.

THE SITUATION WHERE THEY ARE CONVENIENT. Their location can save you time and travel expenses. However, you can focus on states, regions, territories, cities, blocks, a particular zip code, or even a single building if it is packed with genuine prospects. It depends on what your service does and who it is aimed at. Your selling costs tend to go *down* when prospects are conveniently located. Your appeal tends to go *up* when you are nearby.

This Is Critical

The steps beyond this point depend for results on the clarity of your definition of your prospects. That definition gives you something "real" to aim at and helps make the steps that follow make more common sense.

For instance, you may want to name particular qualities that will give you a clearer picture of your prospects. Most prospects will buy your service at a certain time and for certain reasons. Those facts can be part of your definition. So can their motivations and the kind of short-term or long-term objectives toward which your service can help. Here is room to jot down your own ideas and start to build your selling program right here and now. Just put down clear definitions of your very best prospects:

_____

_____

_____

_____

_____

A Short Tour

There follows a short tour of *proven* selling tools that you can review and then apply to selling your service on your own. The purpose is to touch on the highlights and provide definitions and information that can help you build a really convincing presentation of your service. The thought is this: review the proven selling tools first and then build steadily one step at a time right here where you have everything in logical order and in one place. Don't kid yourself! You are going to do this your special way because there isn't any other way. This chapter will give you a way to organize your facts and information and some tools to help you do the job. Here are some definitions.

What Are Selling Ideas?

A selling idea is an idea that *focuses* on your prospect's *buying motives*—the real reasons why he or she will buy your service. Now you can see why it is so vital to have a clear definition of your prospects. A good selling idea is simple and it can do several jobs for you. It can create a strong impression on your prospect's imagination. It may help your prospect to realistically associate his or her needs, wants, and future wealth with you and your service. It may touch and move your prospect to take action. Some of the best selling ideas are based on facts—facts found in your service and what it does, facts found in your prospect's job, situation, needs, pressure, market, superiors, competition, economics, short- or long-term purposes. It doesn't pay to guess too much about these things. You can find out about them by interviewing half a dozen real prospects. Look for their buying motives. Sometimes they are obvious—increased sales, recognition, prestige, better use of resources, additional revenue, or a genuine saving. Each situation is different. The best thing to do is ask.

What Are Sales Points?

Sales points are specific advantages or benefits that your prospect gets as a result of your service. It may be more money, more sales, a saving—but these benefits are cited so frequently that they often have no credibility. You have to *translate* the benefits and advantages you offer into satisfactions. It is your prospect's idea of the satisfactions "ahead" that really stimulates action. When those satisfactions are clear, genuine, and credible, your prospect is likely to sell himself or herself. It helps to have a reasonable range of sales points that you understand thoroughly. Then you can use them selectively and adapt to different interests of different prospects.

Can You Make One Promise?

Sometimes you can boil an offer of service down to one convincing and interesting promise of service. Then you can support that promise with sales points, facts, evidence, examples, or values that make the promise clear, convincing, and buyable. The most convincing-*sounding* sales idea, promise, or sales point won't work unless it is backed with convincing evidence. The level of confidence and trust you can generate depends on how convincing your evidence is to your prospect. When that evidence is simple, clear, specific, and truthful, you can expect results from genuine prospects. If it is also stated in easy-to-understand language with persuasive qualities of understatement, you may expect even better results.

Test Your Selling Ideas and Sales Points

Ask yourself: Is this a point I would want or that would satisfy my buying motives if I were in my prospect's shoes? Is it something unique or unusual that I would specially want from my kind of service? Is it something exclusive that he or she can't get anywhere else? Test questions like these can help you to strengthen your selling ideas and information.

Anticipate Prospect's Questions

When you anticipate your prospect's questions in the course of presenting your service, your chances of acceptance go up and you may be able to resolve some "objections" in advance.

The following questions are the result of special research with prospects in large, medium, and small companies who buy a range of professional, business, and specialized services including finance, communications, systems design, law, accounting, and architecture, to touch on a few.

The questions reveal what prospects want to know when someone is offering them a new service for the first time. The first set of questions covers what they want to know when they are "just looking."

Just looking:
1. What does your service do?
2. Does it fill a need of ours?
3. Will it help me to do a better job?
4. Who have you worked for?
5. What have you done for them?
6. Why is your service pertinent to me?
7. Who else in my organization would be interested?
8. Will you be easy and comfortable to work with?
9. Are you being candid and honest with me?
10. Are you clear about what you can and cannot do?
11. Have you done your homework about me?
12. What does your service cost? Will it fit our budgeting levels for your kind of work?
13. Do you have knowledge and experience we don't have on staff . . . or might need soon or in the near future?
14. Will you get along with some of my associates?

Really interested:
1. What is the real problem?
2. Why can't we do it ourselves?
3. Who will do the work?

4. Will the results really help me?
5. Will I get my money's worth?
6. What will it cost?
7. Who is responsible on your side?
8. Who is responsible on our side?
9. Are you competent? Will you really do it?
10. Will you do it without pushing and shoving from me?
11. When will you start? When will I get results?
12. What will others think?

These are typical spoken and unspoken questions that occur to prospects during a call. You may be able to work answers to some of them into your presentation to make it more interesting and convincing to your prospects.

Answer Objections

First, consider the obvious objections that you would expect or that you have used yourself on occasion. *I don't have the time.* Toss in your most urgent benefit or satisfaction and suggest alternative times for an appointment. *I'm too busy.* Try to get the prospect to agree that he or she is never too busy to look at a service that will produce additional profit (or similar benefits) and then ask them for a ten-minute appointment. *I'm not interested.* Ask the reason why. When you get it, try to respond convincingly to that reason. *I'll think it over.* Again, find out why. This might bring to the surface a real objection that accounts for evident hesitation. *I have to consult with . . .* He or she might be thinking of a partner or a boss. Suggest that the partner or boss will want full information and arrange an appointment to provide that information.

Obviously, there are a number of standard objections you may run across and it is quite practical to recognize them and work out simple, clear, and direct answers that will move your sale forward. You can identify and answer beforehand these more obvious objections because they come up often. Try to answer them during the presentation of your service and thus defuse them.

Second, there are the unexpected objections that arise naturally. They can come from anywhere including left field. Look at them as evidence that your prospect doesn't understand your presentation and really needs more information. This attitude will take some of the sting out of negative reactions. Keep going and use the technique of public speakers. When an unexpected objection arises, turn it into a question and answer it. Sometimes you can answer an objection in a way that strengthens your presentation. Some objections are really indications that your prospect is about ready to buy your service but is resisting the act of making the decision. He or she might say, "I wish I could . . ." This is the time to empathize and reassure your prospect that he or she is doing the right thing. There are many excellent books on selling which go into more detail about the correct ways to handle objections that you might like to look into. Here some of the highlights are presented as useful working tools when you sell your service.

State Your Price

When you carefully plan and place the statement of the price of your service in your presentation, your chances of acceptance actually go up. Your prospective client can't buy your service unless he or she knows the approximate cost. If you avoid stating your price, your prospect is likely to think it is too high. Your prospect probably equates the results he or she wants, to some degree, with your estimate or price. The statement of your price should be realistically related to those results . . . to what your service produces . . . to what your service helps your client to produce. With many professional and specialized services, the price is often related to a particular solution to a particular problem, so you can feel free to be specific.

Convince yourself first. Decide on a fair price to your prospect for the *results* you will deliver—a price that covers your time and expenses and that will yield a fair profit. You must believe that it is a fair price if you expect to sell it convincingly. Fair to you. Fair to your client. Then . . . stick to it. You are really setting a price on the results your client gets in connection with the specific problem he or she wants you to solve.

Pick Your Timing

There is no single way to time or place the statement of your price in the presentation of your service. One occasion when a price can be stated logically is after a clear demonstration of the value of your service. If you are working with a high price you may want to state it early so that your prospect will get used to the idea. Follow that early statement with a clear demonstration of advantages, benefits, or satisfactions that make the high price worth it.

Quote your price when *you* feel the timing is right. The important thing is to plan for it and be ready to fit it in effectively according to the situation. If you believe your price is fair, you can quote it confidently, which is critical to creating confidence in your prospect.

Watch Your Attitudes

It is important to demonstrate that you are thinking, talking, and acting in your client's best interests. You must believe that your price is fair or you won't be able to convince anyone. Remember, however, that people who are knowledgeable about prices and fees believe that most prospects will accept the most expensive service when they are convinced they will get their money's worth.

The real job is to convince your prospect of the value of your service in direct relationship to what he or she wants to accomplish. Demonstrate and show precisely how your service can help your prospect to accomplish his or her specific purposes.

Handle Your Price Convincingly

Pick an approach or combination of approaches that convinces you first and then fit them into the presentation of your service until you feel comfortable. Here are some specifics.

1. Emphasize what your prospect will get in terms of the satisfaction of his or her buying motives . . . expectations . . . or achievement of special purposes or objectives. That's what your prospect is really paying for.

2. Explain what you are going to do step-by-step as a way of emphasizing the quality and value of your service. This approach can also make the content of your service clearer to prospects who are not familiar with it.

3. Make your price seem reasonable. Use words like *merely . . . only . . . surprisingly modest . . .* to indicate that your price really is reasonable.

4. A practical tactic to make a high price seem reasonable is simply to suggest a higher price for similar service so that your price sounds low by comparison. You might say something casual like this: "Wouldn't you expect to pay at least $5,000 for this service? Yet, it is only $3,500." Something like that.

5. Bring out the special, exclusive, or one-of-a-kind qualities that give your prospect *clear* benefits and advantages. These "ex-

clusives" can make your service different and more valuable thus making it worth the price.

6. If true, suggest that the results of your work will be of value to several people in his or her organization, thus increasing its evident value.

7. If true, demonstrate that your service can save your prospect time or money, help to do a better job, or increase revenue.

8. If true, suggest that your service will save the time of important people in your prospect's organization, resolve a difficult problem objectively, help to meet special demands in time and on time.

9. If true, suggest that your service tends to pay for itself with the first use of the results you will deliver and that subsequent use increases benefit and value over a long period of time.

10. If true, suggest that the quality of the results you will produce will be remembered long after the price is forgotten.

11. If true, make clear the savings your service will offer. Put it into dollars and cents in a lump sum, or a daily, weekly, or monthly amount—whatever fits your situation.

12. If true, emphasize savings in such intangibles as less wear and tear on your client, the elimination of errors, the passing of responsibility to you, the reduction of pressure on your client from a demanding superior or customer.

Answer Your Prospect's Price Objections

If true, suggest that the price of your service is justified by the quality you deliver and show evidence that proves it.

If true, suggest that price is always relative, that your price is lower than some of your competition when overhead, benefit programs, and other costs are considered versus your own cost. Does your client want to pay for *their* benefit programs on top of everything else?

If true, suggest that you *could* offer your service at a lower price but that experience shows that a lower price would not give satisfaction—that in fact, less expensive services generally produce complaints and problems. If you are in direct competition with a less expensive service, you might casually add that "they know what their service is worth."

If true, suggest that your prospect is really buying top-level performance and that your performance is the result of your years of experience and specialized know-how that can and will produce results quickly and reliably.

If true, suggest that the pricing policy of his or her own business allows for a fair and reasonable profit, and that you have priced your service in the same practical way. You can add that your prospect wouldn't expect to reduce his or her price and you can't reduce yours for the same reasons.

A fair and reasonable way of handling the question of your price during the presentation of your service can move you a long way toward the acceptance of your service. The preceding suggestions aim at helping you to establish a sound working tool when it comes to handling your price convincingly.

Close Your Sale

When you have several ways to "close the sale" of your service, your chances of acceptance are enhanced. The most practical way to close the sale of your service is on the basis of your prospect's reason for going ahead in *his or her* words. Then you can be sure that your prospect agrees and understands.

Until you find his or her motivation or reason for going ahead you can't close the sale. It is your prospect's sense of urgency that does it. Your own sense of urgency will be interpreted as pressure.

When you do find that motivation for going ahead, you can use a specific closing technique to "prompt" him or her to go ahead. A technique that suits you ... suits him or her ... suits the situation and caliber of your prospect.

You can also work "trial closes" into your proposal of service to help your prospect get used to the idea of accepting your service. Here are six standard closes. They fit in naturally after you have made a strong point. Look them over, pick one or two that you like, and learn to make them work for you.

A FIRST STEP CLOSE. This involves little or no risk. It simply means that you suggest that you begin the assignment by taking the first step in executing it. This could be something like starting the research or developing the first rough solutions or ideas. This can be an economical way for a new prospect to try out your service on his or her problems. At the same time, you can get involved. Your prospect gets the project started and there is no undue strain on anyone. This approach can fit almost any situation.

THE ASSUMPTIVE CLOSE. This can also seem quite casual. It is as though you were accepting the obvious. It is more a confirmation of his or her decision to go ahead. It "assumes" that the project is going ahead. It is a very low-pressure approach. It can be used in almost any situation without offending anyone. Yet, if you turn out to be wrong, it will look like a slight misunderstanding on your part. You are free to go ahead and continue to sell your service.

CHOOSE A MINOR POINT. This is also an easily adjustable way to close your sale. It simply recognizes that some people hate to make direct decisions of any kind. You can make their acceptance of your service easier for them by asking them to agree to a minor point or question. Then you treat their agreement as acceptance of your service. For instance, you might agree on the date of the next meeting when you will get information you need or come in with your first visible results. You might seek agreement on how a particular part of the assignment is going to be handled. This approach avoids a direct decision on "the whole thing," which some people prefer to shy away from. The net result: your prospect becomes a client and gets some action; you get some activity. There is little or no pressure.

TAKE PHYSICAL ACTION. There is a certain authority about physical action that seems to fascinate people. They have to take some action themselves to stop your action. With this approach, you start taking some action that your prospect must either "stop" or else consent to by accepting your service. For instance, you might ask to use your prospect's telephone to arrange a meeting with someone outside who would do part of the work on the project. You might start writing down his or her objective as you understand it and show it for approval. You might just stand up and say that you think you can just "make it" to the library to get agreed-upon information. You use some factor involved in a "first-step" as the focus for the action.

LOOK INTO HIS OR HER FUTURE. Here you might use something that is coming up in your prospect's future as the reason for going ahead now. Perhaps, your work has to be completed by a certain time so that your prospect can take it to an industry meeting, which offers a valid reason for starting now. If he or she doesn't accept your service now, it may be too late or something important and obviously wanted might be missed. If you know of an event that puts a "timetable" on your assignment, it can help to prompt an immediate acceptance.

YOU SUM UP. Here you simply summarize the most important benefits, advantages, or satisfactions your prospect gets. You state them in 1, 2, 3 fashion. They "add up" and the combined impact may stimulate your prospect to take action that lets you begin your assignment.

A fair and comfortable way to handle the close of your sale provides you with a valuable tool that can move the acceptance of your service ahead.

Ask Questions

Asking questions is another basic tool that can help you get the information you need to evaluate a prospect's interest in your service. The fact is that professional and specialized services are often vague and abstract by their very nature. The content of your service may seem obvious enough to you but you can't rely on every prospect understanding it. In fact, many good prospects are themselves experts in many subjects but may not happen to know your subject area at all. They may not need to since they can hire you. As some genius put it: If it can be misunderstood it will be. This fact can be a critical point in the sale of professional or specialized services to prospects who don't understand them.

It is here that the art of asking questions can help you. When you ask prospects questions and they do most of the talking both of you can see more clearly where, when, and how your offer of service fits into the situation.

MAKE YOUR PURPOSE CLEAR. Your prospect will want to know why you are asking questions and what you are going to do with the answers. Tell your prospect frankly that you want to find out if your service fits his or her needs and whether it would really be of value. Start with a few questions to find out what your prospect knows about your kind of service. Find out what is happening in your prospect's organization where your service would fit. Get your prospect to talk.

REACT TO WHAT HE OR SHE SAYS. This is a powerful tool that encourages response and helps to get to the point more quickly. It helps to listen for and encourage expressions of feeling from your prospect . . . however faint. Respond with a smile. This will offer your prospect encouragement. It can help to ask questions like these: Can you expand on that? What do you have in mind? What do you see ahead short-term? You are offering reassurance and getting information at the same time. You are also approaching your prospect as an individual. Most of us want this kind of attention.

USE SIMPLE QUESTIONS. Try to avoid preconceived ideas about what your prospect's answers should be. Get natural answers. Make the answers important and encourage your prospect to keep going. The simple question "For instance?" can often open up useful examples and information. Other questions: What is the real problem? What is the cause of the problem? What are you doing now that works best? A few well-planned questions will often open up floodgates of information, helpful in judging the desirability of your prospect and useful in the immediate performance and delivery of your service.

The End of the Short Tour

This has been a short tour of proven selling techniques. There are many excellent books on selling that will go into much more detail. The purpose here is limited to covering some of the highlights so that you can use them to develop a sales presentation about your service that will really work.

Build a Convincing Presentation

This means convincing to you and to your prospects, in that order. Convince yourself that an orderly, logical presentation of your service can make *all* the difference to the level of understanding and acceptance you can get. Indeed, it can put you in control of the sale of your service.

Consider the alternative: a stumbling, disjointed, and disorganized presentation that your prospects have trouble understanding and a hard time buying. Or, an endless series of "conversations" with prospects that produce no visible results except your own continuing frustration.

As you work along, you will learn more and more about what you have to sell and precisely how to sell it. You can be assured in advance that most prospects will be impressed when they see that you have taken the trouble to organize your presentation to make it easy for them to understand and buy.

You can expect increasing confidence as you develop a really flexible grasp of your presentation. Then, you will begin to enjoy freedom to be yourself in front of new prospects while, at the same time, concentrating on each prospect as an individual. You will be increasingly relaxed and convincing.

As you will see, this approach moves one step at a time and builds up to give you genuine control of each call on a new prospect and solid control of the sale of your service.

You can believe that a thoroughly prepared presentation of your service that will convince you first is far more likely to convince your prospects as well. When you lay the content, benefits, and advantages of your service on the table, your prospect knows that you have confidence in it and this will give him or her confidence in you and what you are saying.

Collect Your Evidence

This step is limited to just collecting your special evidence in one place. Evidence that supports your proposition of service will make it convincing to your prospects. Here are examples of the kind of evidence that most people like, understand, and accept. Nobody has it all! Just work from your strengths.

1. Personal experience
2. Examples of your work
3. Statistics and facts
4. Judgment of third-party experts regarding the value of your kind of service
5. Analogies or parallels that make the value of your service clear
6. Demonstrations
7. Organized information
8. Special resources
9. Special contacts
10. Evidence of results
11. Case histories
12. Problem solutions
13. Graphs and charts
14. Testimonials
15. Experience in your prospect's kind of business
16. Names of people he or she would know
17. Names of important users of your service

You might like to start putting this evidence together here so that you can use it later in your presentation. The first step is to get it down on paper where you can use it and start to really build. Here's room to start your special collection of evidence.

Collect Your Evidence

_____

_____

_____

_____

_____

List Your Facts

This means facts that make your service credible and buyable, facts about the extent of your service, facts about what your service does, facts about what your service will enable your prospect to do or accomplish.

Don't overlook your prospect and his or her special situation. This is where your clear definition of your prospect can work hard for you. Explore the facts of your prospect's situation: Facts about what he or she faces, facts about the competitive situation, facts about competitors, facts about your prospect's position in the industry, sales record, short- or long-term needs. Look at your prospect's annual report, advertising, and sales promotion for background.

Don't forget the current business cycle. There may be facts there that can help you, facts about what's happening in your prospect's industry that affect the long- or short-term results he or she can get. You may identify a situation where your service can help your prospect to get results despite the current business cycle. For instance, if there's a "tight money" market and your service can help, you have a natural entrée that should interest your prospect.

List Your Facts

_____

_____

_____

_____

_____

Sift Your Experience

This means experience that is directly relevant to the performance of your service. This kind of personal experience is enormously convincing and believable. It can quickly improve your chances of acceptance.

Jot down your working credentials. Who have you worked for? What have you done for them? What about the results of your work? What about experience in your prospect's kind of business?

Jot down a list of special assignments, jobs, or projects you have worked on in the past which seem to have a genuine relationship to your prospect's needs and problems.

Look over your experience for special contacts, information sources, and similar background that can help make your service convincing and competitive.

Examine your special knowledge which has a direct impact on the results you can get for your prospects, your special know-how that you can rely on and that will produce visible results. This is the kind of raw material that forms a reliable basis for the content of your presentation. The purpose here is to bring enough of it together in one place where it is easily accessible to you. You may never have to use it all. But you have to have it available when you need it during a presentation. Knowing it is there can make a lot of difference to your own confidence when you are in front of your prospects.

Sift Your Experience

_____

_____

_____

_____

_____

Define the Values

Identify the intangible values that can give your service special believability or prestige. These values can reassure your prospect with regard to the _safety_ of accepting your service and they demonstrate the quality he or she can expect from you. Your prospect can point to these values to offset criticism from others. Convincing values can also help your prospects to accept your service when they are not familiar with its content and must buy on the basis of faith in you.

You may find practical values in your own background: for instance, your previous associations, your previous record of performance, an organized fund of knowledge or specialized information which demonstrates that you can get the job done, a reputation for being able to do a job without pushing and shoving from a client. In fact, this willingness to do the job can be a decisive value when other qualities in the situation are about equal.

Sometimes, it is possible to identify values from your prospect's viewpoint and present them tactfully as values your service can deliver. This can be very convincing.

In some situations, for instance, there is value in your taking over responsibility for a problem where sticky politics is involved. Your ability to produce results which will take pressure off your prospect from superiors, clients, customers, and other sources is a value which can prompt early acceptance of your service.

Your ability to produce specific results because of knowledge and experience that your prospect doesn't have on staff is another value that can influence acceptance. Your ability to quickly recognize and understand your prospect's situation or problem and respond to it professionally is a value of the "he understands me and my problem and situation" variety that can earn acceptance for you. Your frank, direct, and useful comments about the problem which demonstrate that you are interested in solving the problem, not just making a sale, is another value that can help.

The purpose here is to prompt your own recognition of special values you may truthfully offer your prospects—values which can influence them to accept your service and help you overcome the prejudices which some prospects hold with regard to the "risk" of hiring one person versus a "safe" and recognized team or company. A *few* values like this that are convincing to you and stated in a few sentences may do wonders for you. Here is some room to jot some down.

Define the Values

_____

_____

_____

_____

_____

Define the Benefits

Identify the benefits or advantages your prospect can expect when your service is completed. Most prospects want to know this before they buy a service. Here's a dictionary definition of a benefit or advantage: anything contributing to the improvement in condition . . . a favorable position . . . a gain or superiority.

Standard benefits like an increase in sales, the development of more revenue, or a saving of time need more and more evidence to make them believable. Almost everyone mentions these benefits and many sophisticated buyers have become more and more skeptical. They are useful if you can prove them.

Here are some additional sources of benefits that may help make your service stand out from the crowd. The reason why your kind of service exists may contain a benefit you can use with conviction. The physical results of your service may contain benefits. The timing and convenience of your service may contain benefits. A saving of unreasonable amounts of trial and error because of your service may provide benefits. The control your service provides in an area your prospect is unfamiliar with may provide benefits. A few really convincing benefits you believe yourself can go a long way in reassuring your prospect and encouraging him or her to accept your service. Here's room to jot down your ideas as you go along.

Define the Benefits

_____

_____

_____

_____

_____

Choose Your Satisfactions

Consider the satisfactions your prospect can expect from the use of your service. They are a vital part of what your prospect is buying from you and can be the spark that stimulates him or her to take action—once he or she is convinced of your credentials and the quality of your service. Your chances of early acceptance go up rapidly when you can offer and deliver genuine satisfaction and prove it before hand. Here's a dictionary definition of satisfaction: the fulfillment of needs, expectations, wishes, or desires. The meeting of requirements. Freedom from doubt or anxiety. A convincing solution.

Here the purpose is to define some of the satisfactions you can deliver. They are intangible qualities that your prospect can recognize and relate to easily. Here are some general sources of satisfaction that can stimulate action: your service may offer your prospect a way to take action on his or her own ideas; help to accomplish specific purposes or objectives in time to reap desired rewards; offer a solution to a problem that has been nagging for a long time; help to earn recognition (through your work) from superiors, customers, or clients.

A definition of what your work enables your prospect to accomplish himself or herself can be satisfying. So can the way your work relieves your prospect of pressure or responsibility. The purpose here is to define a few genuine satisfactions you know you can deliver easily that will also be convincing to your prospect. Here's room to jot them down as they appear. You only need a few!

Choose Your Satisfactions

Pick Your Exclusives

In a competitive situation where your service looks and sounds like your competitors', your chances of acceptance can go up when you are able to include genuine exclusives or one-of-a-kind qualities that produce visible results for your prospect. These exclusive qualities set your service apart from your competition and can make it more desirable to a prospect.

You may find exclusive or one-of-a-kind qualities in your personal experience. They may be in your special knowledge. They could be in the special contacts you have. They may be in a combination of knowledge and experience. They might involve a special skill or know-how that lets you produce quick results. They may be in your ability to provide background information which enables your prospect to make more comfortable decisions in an unfamiliar area. They might be in a particular chunk of relevant experience that matches what your prospect is doing. They may be in the fact that you "have been there before" and can help your prospect avoid costly mistakes. They may be in the formal credentials which are essential in your field—only yours are different and better than others. The fact is that a small exclusive can make a lot of difference to the acceptance of your service. Here's room to jot some down for use later.

Pick Your Exclusives

_____

_____

_____

_____

_____

Get Some Help

You can strengthen the quality of your selling ammunition by involving qualified friends, associates, or even prospects as you develop your offer of service for selling purposes. Suggest to them that you would like to review the feasibility of an approach to selling your service. You may get a lot of useful information, ideas, objective viewpoints, and usable feedback that can really help. You may also be alerted to unproven assumptions or the kind of subjectivity that can seriously throw you off the track, and avoid these pitfalls.

When it comes to preparing your presentation and any supporting materials, it may help to call on a few professional writers, designers, or marketing people. Hire them as consultants. There is nothing more difficult than writing about your own service. Their objectivity can help and then all you need do is edit their work to suit your situation as you see it. The facts and information you have gathered to this point is what they need to work with.

What Is a Sales Presentation?

The real point of all selling is to stimulate a prospect to buy something. A sales presentation fits into this context. It is a logically organized and convincing talk that moves from the opening right through to the acceptance of your service. It is complete and thorough whether you need to use it all in front of a given prospect or not. *Knowing* that your complete story is available enables you to use it with confidence, flexibility, and control. You can easily adapt it to different prospects, prospect reactions, or prospect needs and situations. But you have to have it first before you can adapt it. That's what the work to this point has been all about.

A sales presentation is logically organized around a proven selling format (just ahead) so that you can understand and remember it easily and your prospect can "get it" just as easily. You can control the course of the sales call. You can be quietly confident in the bargain because you *do* know what you are going to say and do have a firm grip on your own story.

Some Useful Qualities

A convincing sales presentation focuses on your prospect's buying motives. It brings out the values, benefits, and satisfactions he or she can expect. It answers obvious questions about you and your qualifications. It talks facts instead of theory. It tells the truth and addresses each prospect at his or her level and in his or her language. It uses understatement instead of overstatement. It makes conservative promises that are more believable and easier to keep later than exaggerated claims. It uses sales ideas, sales points, and solid reasons for the acceptance of your service.

Your presentation is aimed at and *dedicated* to each prospect's interests, needs, and wants . . . one at a time. This kind of approach can create an enormous change in a genuine prospect's attitudes toward you and your service. The prospect experiences that change. This is precisely what makes this kind of presentation convincing. Remember, your service is intangible, abstract, and may be vague to many prospects. Acceptance may call for a certain amount of faith, confidence, and belief on his or her part. He or she may be an expert in a particular field but not familiar with yours. Put yourself in your prospect's shoes. Aim at a specific prospect whose qualifications you have defined earlier in this chapter. In fact, get that definition out and put it in front of you to help you keep track. Now, you are aiming at someone specific and the job of preparing your presentation will make more common sense.

Two Critical Problems

Many professional and specialized services need to be introduced to new prospects clearly and convincingly. They are seldom accepted on the first call. In fact, they are accepted *only* when a prospect needs them. The timing of acceptance is on the prospect's side in terms of the needs of the moment. This influences the content of a sound introductory sales call on a new prospect. It also helps define the specific purpose of that call: to gain the prospect's confidence and trust, then find out what he or she wants or expects from your kind of service. This gives you a way to "measure" your sales call before your start.

A second fact that influences the content of the introductory sales call is that professional and specialized services are abstract and hard to understand. To many prospects they are vague. Your prospects may be experts in their fields but know little or nothing about yours. It doesn't pay to take anything for granted on this point. It does pay to use simple visual aids whenever you can to make what your service does and can do for your prospect crystal clear. This can save you a lot of guesswork and misunderstanding which can delay acceptance of your service.

With your specific prospect in mind and the selling information you have gathered to this point, let's take a look at a proven format for a sales call. Then you can see a way to organize your information for selling purposes. This step puts the information in logical sequence. You can sharpen it later.

Two Useful Sales Tools

When you *show* evidence that supports what you say, your chances of convincing your prospect go up. Why? Because eyes are far more effective in registering ideas than ears. Seeing increases the chances of understanding enormously compared with listening for the same length of time.

In fact, the more of his or her senses you can involve in your presentation the more likely he or she is to understand it and you. This is particularly vital when you are seeing an important prospect who can give you only a limited amount of time. It is also important when you feel that he or she will be unfamiliar with your kind of service yet you need understanding, faith, and belief to make your service easy to buy.

Tell your prospect what you are going to show *before* you

show it so that he or she is prepared. Tell what to look for so that you can be sure that he or she gets the points you want to get across. Make every effort to personalize your evidence to your prospect's situation so that it is clear where and how your service fits and can be useful.

A simple way to visualize your service is through a standard presentation book. This means you develop a step-by-step guide through your presentation going from page to page so that you can present your service in a logical sequence. Be sure to keep the book in *your* hands so that your prospect doesn't peek ahead and get confused. Make your sales points about the content of each page. Ask questions to see if he or she really understands what you are showing.

The content will depend on your service. But here are some suggestions to consider: written case histories, clear problem solutions, photographs showing the need or "before and after" treatments, charts, graphs, pertinent magazine articles that demonstrate third-party endorsement of the need, testimonials, examples of your work that tie into his or her situation and demonstrate the relevance of your service. Give your presentation book a title. It could begin like this: A service that . . . or A program that . . . followed by what it does for your prospect. Don't overlook the convincing possibilities of visualizing your service to make it stand out from your competition.

When you demonstrate your service, your chances of getting understanding of it go up dramatically. A demonstration can make your service visible, tangible, and interesting to your prospect A demonstration should be based on your prospect's needs or buying motives. Visualization and demonstration can tell your prospect more in half the time it would take in words alone . . . and more clearly, dramatically, and memorably. A demonstration is really a dramatic act that has a strong impact on your prospect so that he or she will remember it for a long time. It also helps to create a high level of interest. It will work even better if you can get your prospect into your act by asking questions about how your service fits his or her needs. A demonstration lets your prospect see your service in action, which shows your confidence and arouses your prospect's interest. Some services lend themselves to this kind of treatment and others don't. It depends on what your service is and how you feel about "performing" like this.

The way you visualize your service and the materials you use to support what you say should be developed with professionalism.

Don't hesitate to call on consultants who can help you with the planning, writing, design, and preparation of these key materials and save your own time for other important jobs.

A Service Sales Call

Here is a proven format to arrange the elements of your presentation in logical sequence for selling purposes. You can put your information under these headings and make the basic content of your presentation fall into place.

Incidentally, you may want to look at page 76 to see what new prospects want to know about you and your service when they are just looking. If you are working with a clear definition of your prospect in front of you, this step will make more sense to you because you are aiming at someone specific—not at thin air. Here we are also aiming at a new prospect who is a stranger, so the information needs about you and your service are more extensive and you are more likely to cover all the needed information. Here is the proven sales format. They are really steps in a process.

1. Opening
2. Attract his or her attention
3. Attract his or her interest
4. Earn his or her confidence
5. Earn his or her trust
6. Find out what he or she wants

This is about all you can do on a first call on a new prospect. Your purpose is to find out if the prospect is a good one, who will be worth further investment of your time and develop into a paying client.

Open Your Sales Call

You can open your sales call and attract your prospect's attention at the same time. Open your call naturally with a courteous introduction that gives your name and helps to set the tone of the meeting. That's the first thing to jot down. Then you might ask your prospect's name in the form of a question to be sure that you are talking to the right person.

The first seconds of a sales call set the tone so that what you say *next* deserves special consideration. Your second sentence aims at converting him or her into an attentive and interested listener. What it says should be comfortable for you and in character with your prospect and his or her situation.

Here are some ways to "open" that can help attract your prospect's attention. Look them over to see if you find one that fits your situation. You don't need much—one or two may just do it for you. Tell your prospect what your service will *do* in a sentence or two. Ask a thought-provoking question, something that relates to your prospect's situation, interests, business, how he or she is doing or likely to do. Tell the kind of problem you can solve and that you would like to show examples of your work and results. Show your examples and put your prospect's eyes to work. Perhaps you can make one emphatic and interesting promise or name a particular benefit that you can back up to the hilt. Then tell your prospect that you are going to show evidence that backs up that promise. Perhaps you can find a news item about the current business cycle that backs up the need for your kind of service. Offer it as a third-party or impartial justification for your kind of service.

These are a few starting points for your review. Here is room to jot down what you want to use so that you can begin to build your presentation.

Open Your Sales Call

_____

_____

_____

_____

_____

Arouse His or Her Interest

When you turn your prospect into an attentive listener or looker you dramatically increase your chances of acceptance. What you say next about the benefits and advantages that your service can deliver should be specific, clear, brief, and to the point. Remember, your prospect has other things to do. You are a guest in his or her office. Here are some ways to arouse interest. See if some of them are comfortable for you and fit your prospect's special interests and needs.

Choose specific values, benefits, advantages, and satisfactions that will fit the largest number of prospects you have in mind. Tell your prospects about them in a few words each. For instance, you might point out the basic need for your service if you feel that he or she is unfamiliar with it. You can personalize the benefits to your prospect's situation and make it easier for him or her to relate to what you are saying. You can ask questions to determine whether or not you are being understood. Questions involve your prospect and can help you both determine where and if your service fits his or her situation. If true, show that your service is best for his or her special needs and situation (as you understand it) by using some of those exclusive or one-of-a-kind qualities that prove it. The more your prospect says *yes* the more unreasonable an arbitrary turndown will seem to him or her later on. Here is some room to jot down your own ideas.

Arouse His or Her Interest

_____

_____

_____

_____

_____

Earn His or Her Confidence

Demonstrate that you are thinking, acting, and talking entirely in your prospect's interest. Show that you want him or her to get maximum value from your service and that you will protect his or her interests all along the line. Make your offer of service as free of problems as you possibly can. You don't have to make a perfect case. There probably isn't one anyway. But it is important that your attitudes show throughout and that the excellence and relevance of your work are visible and clear. It is qualities like this that can elicit your prospect's confidence. Here are some specific ways to arouse confidence. Select some that fit your situation as you see it.

Show facts and figures that demonstrate the value of the results of your service. Tell your prospect an analogy or parallel that makes your service clear. Tell what your prospect will be able to do or get as a result of your service. Show concrete evidence: examples, charts and graphs, a case history, a problem solution. Tell about your experience in his or her field so that your prospect will know that he or she won't have to spend hours explaining things to you. Show testimonials from people your prospect knows who are in similar situations and hold similar jobs. Work from your special evidence and strengths. Nobody has it all! Here is room to write in some of your strengths and keep moving.

Earn His or Her Confidence

_____

_____

_____

_____

_____

Earn His or Her Trust

Many knowledgeable prospects react to the attitudes of people whose services they use even more than they do to the facts. It can boil down to your prospect's feeling about you and your service. When a prospect faces choices of services which are about equal it can come down to his or her gut feeling. For instance, whether your prospect likes or trusts you, a "reading" about whether or not you would be comfortable to work with, his or her reaction as to whether or not you were candid and honest, impressions about how well you would get along with your prospect's associates. These intangibles can be decisive in the final choice from your prospect's side of the desk.

What can you do about them? You can take a look at your attitudes. Here are some for review that can have a genuine impact. They can make a big difference when you are seeking clients with whom you want to develop a long-term relationship. These viewpoints are suggested for review only and as possible goals. You are the sole judge. These suggestions aim at simultaneously building your morale and your prospect's trust. Pick up whatever feels right to you and toss out the rest since they won't work for you.

Adopt the firm belief that your best interests are _always_ served by protecting your prospect's interests. If he or she is unfamiliar with your service, help to make the best and right choices in light of the situation.

Give your prospect information he or she can use and trust in making the choice to accept or not accept your service. Perhaps the project involved is more than you can handle on your own. If so, say so. This viewpoint can stimulate trust and may open sound opportunities in the future. This kind of viewpoint can put your heart in the right place, making it easier for you to say and do the right things which will earn your prospect's confidence and trust.

Accept the idea that selling your service is important and learn your selling story so well that you are not inhibited about it and can gain the freedom from it to focus your full attention on each prospect as an individual and one at a time.

Consider the idea that any real progress you make will come about because your prospect trusts you and, through your performance, wants you to succeed.

Develop and maintain a clear picture of yourself succeeding as you enter each new sales call and keep sharpening that picture as you go along to maintain your own confidence and morale.

The idea of giving more than you expect to get can make you stand out from the competition and encourage the trust and acceptance of people who can make your service a permanent success. Here's some room to jot down any ideas that appeal to you and seem workable from your viewpoint.

Earn His or Her Trust

_____

_____

_____

_____

_____

Find Out What He or She Wants

This is a critical step in the successful sale of many professional and specialized services. Very frequently, the buyer who is unfamiliar with your service doesn't really know what he or she wants or should want because of that unfamiliarity. You can help your prospect by asking questions about the situation that can help you both to determine where and if your service will really help.

When a prospect has a reasonable idea of your background, the benefits and advantages of your particular service, and what your service can and cannot do, he or she is in a better position to determine its value in his or her special situation. A few quiet and encouraging questions from you can bring information to light that can help you both to make a better judgment of where and how you might be of service. He or she won't open up until you have established confidence and trust, which is one of the purposes of the preceding steps.

Here are some questions that might help you as a starting point. Ask your prospect: What do you want to accomplish? What is the problem? What is the *cause* of the problem? This question can sometimes reveal both the problem itself and a self-evident objective. When your prospect unfolds his or her special situation the simple query "For instance?" can help to uncover useful points. The idea of questions is simply to get your prospect to do most of the talking so that you can see when, if, and where your service fits. The more your prospects talk, the more convincing you look to them. This is a good time to jot down some questions you want to use.

Find Out What He or She Wants

_____

_____

_____

_____

_____

Make Your First Draft

Bring together the information you have written down to this point, using the format of a sales call as your basic outline.

Then add in your brief answers to obvious objections, a clear statement of your price, and the kind of "sales close" that you feel will work best for you. With the addition of these key elements you will have a more complete picture for selling purposes of what your service offers. This means the basic substance of your story. The purpose is to keep it as simple as possible and understand it yourself first.

Each prospect's situation is different. With some you may use a tiny bit of your total presentation and only the questions that encourage your prospect to talk about his or her situation. With others you may want to use the entire presentation. The purpose is to *have* it so that you can use it flexibly according to each situation. Some prospects will be more knowledgeable about your kind of service than others, so you can safely skip some of the pieces of your story. Make sure that your offer of service is right before you put a lot of money into supporting materials. Make sure that your presentation satisfies your prospect's natural desire to be treated with respect as an individual. Don't upstage anyone with technical words or a superior attitude. Use the word "you" whenever you sensibly can. Most activities have their own trade words which can help you when you are talking to a prospect who would expect you to know them. Whenever possible, use dramatic, concrete, and vivid words; very specifically, words that stand for things your prospect can see, feel, and touch. This will help you increase the impact and meaning of what you say. It can also help you stimulate understanding on your prospect's side of the desk. The chief communication in a sales presentation is through the spoken word. That's why sharpening the words of your presentation can make a big difference in the acceptance you get. Try to keep everything as brief and to the point as possible.

Remember Your Presentation

When you remember the content of your presentation you get a sense of freedom and confidence so that you can concentrate on the most effective delivery to each prospect. Your increased confidence helps to stimulate acceptance. Remembering your presentation also gives you control and flexibility. You can move away from it to respond to unexpected questions or a change of direction. Then you can move back to it and go ahead. You are in control. The work of preparing your presentation teaches you all about what you are selling and how to sell it. When you remember your presentation you are more likely to cover the key points when you meet a new prospect. This will build up to produce a better likelihood of acceptance.

When you don't remember your presentation in front of new prospects you may give an impression that is disjointed, hard to understand, and difficult to buy. When you really have a sound service that is not being accepted just because it is misunderstood you can see the value of developing an organized way to present your service so that it is easy to remember and deliver.

Here's a simple way to remember your presentation. Memorize the key points in your original outline first. Then memorize what is in between by reading it out loud. This makes the associations or relationships clearer and means that you are remembering fewer units. Those units are also in logical sequence, which makes them even easier to work with.

Here is a way to prepare your sales presentation that is borrowed from a technique used for delivery of speeches:

Type out your presentation on the right-hand two-thirds of a page. Then read it aloud four or five times. Then write "cue words" on the left opposite each paragraph. Those cue words will have special meaning for you. They will bring back the content of each paragraph easily and immediately.

Then fold the paper so that *only* the cue words show and deliver your presentation again. You will find that about 80 percent of the material will come back easily and naturally *in your own words of the moment* . . . not "canned" or memorized. The purpose is to know it well enough so that you can say it easily and in your own words. You don't have to memorize everything and say it exactly that way every time. Knowing it well enough so that you can say it easily and naturally anytime, anywhere, gives you real freedom.

Rehearse your presentation out loud against a radio newscast as a way of getting used to "interference" or the unexpected distractions that can occur when you are in front of a prospect. You can also tape-record your presentation and listen to it to find out what will make it even more effective. During the first few meetings with prospects you may want to keep your presentation script with you to get support from the cue words and the content of some paragraphs.

Rehearsing can help you relax so that you can focus on improving your delivery, your eye contact with prospects, and building or developing the kind of impression that makes you convincing. It is vital to rehearse *out loud.* You can find out which words, phrases, or sentences are awkward for *you* to say. Then you can eliminate them or rewrite them until you are comfortable. Reading out loud will also tell you where the inflections or pauses should be to add interest and emphasis to your delivery. Rehearse in a background as close to the actual conditions as possible—standing up, sitting down, in an office.

Rehearse pauses, inflections, eye contact, and different levels of delivery until they feel entirely natural to you. It is specially important to look your prospect in the eye at the beginning. This makes you more convincing and believable and adds credibility to the delivery of your presentation.

Don't Fall in Love

It's easy to "fall in love" with your own material and have subjective ideas about its effectiveness. The only people who can help you sharpen and improve your presentation are actual prospects. You can make quick progress by setting up ten or twelve meetings with real prospects. This experience will help to rehearse your presentation and get really comfortable with it. When you have finished each call, ask each prospect to help you improve. You may be delightfully surprised at how willingly help may be offered. Here are some questions as a starting point for getting solid information that can help you strengthen your presentation enormously.

1. What is your attitude toward this kind of service?
2. What do you expect from this kind of service personally?
3. What do you expect from this kind of service for your organization?
4. What is your chief motivation for wanting this kind of service?
5. What does this service help you to accomplish?
6. How do you justify the use of this kind of service?
7. How do you justify the cost of this kind of service?
8. What does this service do that helps you most? What's going on then?
9. What are the three most important values you see in this service?
10. What did you want the last time you used this kind of service?
11. Where do you look for this kind of service, when you want it?
12. Who else is involved in your acceptance of this kind of service?
13. What does this service do that you want most?
14. Why do you go outside for this kind of service?

Notice that these questions ask about your "kind" of service, not your specific service. This makes it easier for a prospect to give candid and useful answers. You may be surprised at what you hear. Then you can work the results into your presentation and your way of selling your service.

Record What They Say

It is what prospects say in their words, in everyday language and spontaneously, that will give you reliable clues to their real viewpoint about your presentation and service. Listen carefully. Take notes. Write down the actual words. Then let this information build up until you are satisfied that you have a solid grip on your prospects' viewpoints. You may find, after ten or twelve visits like this, that the answers begin to run together and that the same answers are reappearing. Where they agree you are most likely to be able to rely on the content and put it to effective use in building your selling program.

Move into High Gear

With the way you are going to present your service under reasonable control, you are ready to move into high gear and get your first client. You will find that getting the first client is hard because nobody on the client side wants to be first. You can overcome this with the quality of your presentation and make a real and satisfying breakthrough.

Now is the time to develop the next steps in your selling program, drawing on some of the work done so far and on the content of your presentation.

Let's take a look at your prospect list again—the one that you defined carefully at the beginning of this chapter. Now the problem is to get in and see them. The real problem is to do this in a way that is comfortable for you and will take minimum time. The fact is that some people are marvelously convincing on the telephone. Others prefer to write letters to evaluate a prospect's level of interest before the call. Still others with plentiful contacts prefer to use referrals. All three work and you may want to use all of them. However, if one of them is really "right" for you, it may be best to concentrate on that one until you can make it work effortlessly. It is what you like and do best that counts. It is better to do a few things well than respond to what others do well but you don't.

Make a Phone Call

This is one of the simplest and most direct ways to find out if a specific prospect is interested in your kind of service and will see you. Some of the content of your presentation can be useful here. Plan your call carefully so that what you have to say is specific, brief, and can be covered in about thirty seconds. Make your listener comfortable. Give your name, what your service does or can help your listener to do in a few quick sentences. Your listener needs to know who is talking, why you are calling, and what you want so that he or she can relax. You can arouse interest by mentioning some of the benefits, values, or advantages your service can deliver. But don't reveal too much. The purpose of the call is to arouse interest so that your listener will want to make an appointment with you. Be sure to identify the right person to receive your call before you start to avoid wasting time.

Answer some of his or her questions. But if he or she wants extensive information, suggest that you can't do justice to your service on the telephone (which is probably true) any more than he or she can evaluate it properly on the telephone. Make this the basis for requesting an appointment. Suggest one or two specific times to provide a choice but don't be overeager to meet your prospect's schedule. Try to make your voice pleasant and as friendly as possible. Your voice is your most important "weapon" when you make this kind of telephone call. Be sure you speak slowly enough for convenient listening and be as clear as possible.

Keep score: compare the number of telephone calls you make with the number of appointments you set up so that you can see improvement as you go along. If you pick up some "objections," make note of them. Then work out specific one- or two-sentence answers to those objections and incorporate them in your call when they come up. After a while you should be able to develop a telephone call that works (gets you appointments). If you decide on this approach it will pay you to make it really work. Then you can save a lot of time by reserving a half hour or so each week for making calls to set up appointments and cut your selling time and costs accordingly. Here is some room to plan your telephone call so that you can get started and keep moving.

A Door-opening Telephone Call

_____

_____

_____

_____

_____

Write a Sales Letter

A good sales letter is one of the simplest and most economical ways to find out if a specific prospect is really interested in your kind of service. Some prospects like to get letters first so that they have a starting point. When you have a letter that works you can further simplify your selling program by sending out a specific number each week and then making follow-up calls to confirm appointments. Avoid having your letter arrive on "weekend-oriented" Fridays or Mondays. For instance, if you have a prospect list of one hundred you can set up your letter, have it prepared by a letter shop, and send out five every Monday and plan to make the appointment calls every Thursday morning. With this organized approach you can improve your chances of acceptance and still confine your selling time to those follow-up calls every Thursday morning.

Here are some suggestions that can help you make your letter really work. Your prospect will react to the accuracy of your vision of what he or she wants from your kind of service. The more accurately your letter touches on what he or she wants the more likely you are to get an interview. This doesn't mean that you need a different letter for each prospect. Many prospects will want the same benefits, advantages, or values from your kind of service. Concentrate on the ones that apply to the largest number of prospects.

Here are some other sources of the kind of information that can help you make your sales letter work.

Your prospect will buy your service for certain reasons at a certain time. Put that reason and that time into your letter.

Make a survey of some aspect of his or her business and use the letter to report on the results. This almost never fails.

Draw on the material in your presentation to arouse curiosity, using, perhaps, one piece of information.

Define clearly what you can do for him or her . . . solve a problem, open an opportunity, save time or money in a different or out-of-the-ordinary way.

Use some of the benefits, advantages, or satisfactions that your service offers as a reason why he or she should become involved personally.

People always want to know what other people with their problems are doing to cope with them. If you know, put this in your letter. You are likely to get genuine attention.

Can you tie into the current business cycle or current news? You can get an item about such trends from a professional or trade paper and use it as the basis of your letter. It should be news that relates directly to your prospect's interests, needs, wants, or desires.

The purpose of the letter is to get an appointment and nothing more. Make clear what your reader/prospect is supposed to do or expect. The simplest result: he or she can expect a call from you to make an appointment. You might say that you will call the following Thursday at 9:30 A.M. for an appointment. A single convincing and tested sales letter can cut down your selling time substantially. If letters are right for you, here's some room to get started on yours.

A Door-opening Sales Letter

Get Good Referrals

Referrals are another way to open doors. The result you get depends on your asking the right person to ask the right person at the right level. It also depends on their confidence in each other.

Start with people who have confidence in *you.* Concentrate on people with a wide range of contacts in their daily activity—people like lawyers, bankers, accountants, ministers, or successful salesmen. Don't overlook people who have a specific range of contacts in an area which is also your marketplace.

Make it easy to be referred. Provide specific and useful information about yourself and what you are trying to do. Don't take anything for granted. You can't count on anyone knowing exactly what you do just because you are in a certain field. They are likely to be as vague about you as you may be about them. When you want to develop good referrals, be specific about the people you want to see. Give details such as title, kind of organization, level of responsibility of the prospect you seek, specific kinds of problems where your service can help. This kind of picture will give your potential "door opener" something to work with. Show him or her your prospect list. This may spark some additional suggestions. He or she may even know someone on your list and give you an immediate approval to use his or her name.

Outline your credentials and provide a brief thumbnail sketch of your background. Your credentials might give him or her special confidence in you that will encourage the opening of special doors. You may want to show examples of your work. Your contact will want to be sure that your service will be of genuine interest to anyone he or she sends you to see. Here's some room to jot down names of people you feel can provide genuinely useful referrals. A good referral can sometimes open doors that cannot be opened in any other way. Be sure to "report back" and you may encourage additional referrals.

Some Specific Referral Sources

_____

_____

_____

_____

_____

Do Your Homework

Your chances of acceptance are enhanced when you have _a really good prospect_ and do some homework about him or her. Try to get a clearer picture of the situation and what he or she wants. Consider each really good prospect one at a time.

Here are some sources of information. Look at his or her organi-zation's advertising and see what it says. Look at the public relations material and see what it will show you about what the organization is trying to accomplish. Call the public relations department and ask for copies of the annual report, company publications, and other such material. Examine the annual report to see more clearly how the firm is organized, its departments or divisions, who does what, and the names of the top people. Visit the organization's outlets and get first-hand impressions. Talk to its sales people about their views with regard to the organization's needs, problems, or objectives that fall in your area of interest. Talk to some of the customers and get their reaction to your service as it relates to your prospect.

When you have this kind of information in hand you will have a clearer idea of where your service might fit into your prospect's situ-ation and, perhaps, a more realistic idea of what he or she might want from you right now. When you do this kind of homework and "report" the results, you are almost *guaranteed* to get instant interest.

Make Yourself Convincing

The chances of acceptance will increase when you make a strong and favorable personal impression. Here are some intangible quali-ties that contribute to that impression. They are free! They work!

THE WAY YOU ACT. Don't you prefer to meet with someone who is sincere, warm, courteous, energetic, and vital? Your prospect will judge you on such qualities as you may have judged others in the past. It is what you see on the surface. These qualities are worth cultivating because they can have a direct impact on the impression you make.

THE SOUND OF YOUR VOICE. Try to make your voice tell of your belief, confidence, and conviction about the value of your ser-vice. Try to speak so that your words and manner together convey the real meaning of what you are saying. Try to match your voice and movement to give natural emphasis to important points. Keep your voice natural and in character yet try to vary it occasionally. For instance, talk loud, whisper distinctly, talk softly. This kind of change of pace adds interest to what you are saying. The goal is a warm, confident, and friendly voice that conveys assurance and reassurance.

THE WAY YOU LOOK. Don't you tend to trust people who look you square in the eye? Some believe that this "eye contact" is the strongest single way to control a sales call. You can use it to complement what you say, to help confirm important points, to change emphasis. Good eye contact makes a vital difference to the impression you make and the level of confidence you can arouse in a prospect. The way you look also means your level of energy, interest, and alertness. They combine to create a subtle touch that many people like without really knowing why.

THE WAY YOU LISTEN. Listen with interest. Let your prospect know that you are getting his or her message. Respond with a smile or an agreeing nod of the head. Listen for your prospect's expressions of feeling and respond to them. Listen for his or her wants, interests, needs, motivations, and problems. Use listening to respond to your prospect as an individual and you will substantially strengthen the favorable impression you make.

Make Yourself Comfortable

Here are some ways to relax *just before you walk in* on a new prospect who is a stranger. These are suggested goals.

THINK MORE ABOUT YOUR PROSPECT THAN ABOUT YOURSELF. Turn the tables. The more you think about him or her the less time you will have to think about yourself. Try to visualize what he or she wants—the specific situation, needs, or expectations. Think about how your service might fit his or her needs. This is a natural way to approach a call on a new prospect and it can work exceedingly well to help eliminate self-consciousness.

YOU ARE NOT AS EXPOSED AS YOU THINK. You will "size" each other up at the beginning. It's natural. But it takes only a moment. The truth is that the more interested he or she is in your presentation the more invisible you get. You can also rely on the idea that your prospect is likely to be thinking more about himself or herself than about you.

BORROW THIS IDEA FROM ACTORS. Sometimes they almost physically "shake" themselves before "going on." You can do the same. For instance, take a deep breath and it will relax you as you step into your prospect's office.

RECOGNIZE THE IMPORTANCE OF WHAT YOU ARE DOING. It doesn't pay to exaggerate this, but selling your service effectively has a direct impact on the results you get . . . the security you can enjoy . . . the revenue you can earn. It helps to work at selling your service until you are comfortable doing it. The more relaxed you are, the better results you are likely to get. So learning to sell your service is well worth it.

LOOK AT SELLING YOUR SERVICE AS A PROCESS. This can help take away some of the self-consciousness that can accompany selling yourself and your service. Have enough prospects so that no single situation becomes too important for you. This will help you to approach selling with a dignified perspective and a sense of confidence and control.

STEP IN BOLDLY. Start with a firm, clear voice. You'll be amazed at how a good *start* like this can cut down on your tension and give you a wonderful sense of momentum and command. It can also help you create the right atmosphere and impression in which to do a really good selling job.

Give Yourself Measurements

You can make the sale of your service interesting to you by giving yourself measurements. This can help when there is nobody to cheer you on and gives you a basis for encouraging yourself as you make progress. These are really some goals you may want to use. They aim at helping you to measure your own performance when you make a first call on a new prospect.

- Create a relationship of trust with your own candor and honesty.
- Find out what he or she wants.
- Ask questions that get your prospect to do most of the talking.
- Join your prospect in finding out where, when, how, or if your service really fits his or her special needs and situation.

When you practice a bit and find that you can approach these goals comfortably and still respond to your prospect as an individual you will know that you are making real progress.

Anticipate Your Prospect's Reactions

You may feel more comfortable when you have a way to respond to different kinds of reactions from different kinds of people.

WHEN YOUR PROSPECTS . . .	YOU CAN . . .
Don't seem to be listening	Put their eyes to work by showing visual examples of your work.
Aren't responding	Get them involved by asking questions that require complete answers.
Seem reluctant	Offer reassurances, encouragement, and act with increased confidence.
Quibble about fees	Give specific and clear evidence of value, some of your most convincing benefits, advantages, or satisfactions.
Keep raising objections	Make very conservative statements and prove them with convincing evidence, but don't argue.
Doubt your statements	Try to see things from their viewpoint. Ask questions. Locate the reason for skepticism.
Are unexpectedly interrupted	Stop the presentation of your service and try to make an appointment for another time.
Not your type	Politely withdraw. You can never perform satisfying service when the chemistry is *really* off.

If you define your prospects carefully you may not run into too many unusual types. But there are always a few.

Make Your Decision

Do you want the prospect you have just seen as a client? Would his or her acceptance of your service add to your knowledge, experience, or prestige? What is your candid evaluation of your prospect and his or her situation? Decide whether you want this prospect or not before you invest *more* of your own time and money building a relationship. Here are some additional evaluations.

WHAT ABOUT PERSONAL CHEMISTRY? Do you feel that you could work with him or her? With many professional and specialized services good rapport is vital and can determine whether or not you can deliver satisfactory service. When you have excessively negative impressions, walk away. Why invite frustration?

DOES HE OR SHE NEED YOU? Did you get a feeling that there was a genuine need for your service in your prospect's organization or situation? Perhaps they don't have your skills and background on staff and still have an obvious need. Perhaps they have problems where you can help and they don't have enough people inside to cover. Is there a realistic opportunity for you?

DOES HE OR SHE WANT YOU? Did there seem to be genuine interest in you and your service? Did you feel that this reaction was sincere and positive enough to warrant a belief that he or she would accept your service when the need was there? Or, at the very least, give you an open or competitive opportunity?

CAN HE OR SHE AFFORD YOU? Is the level of your fee or price appropriate to the organization? Are you likely to fit their budgeting levels for your kind of service? This is most likely to be a guess but it is worth making. If the answer is no, you may feel that you should not pursue this particular prospect further.

WILL HE OR SHE PAY YOU? Can your prospect approve the level of your fee or price or must approval be sought upstairs where things might get out of your control? Does the organization have a sound credit rating? Your judgment on these points may influence your next steps with a given prospect.

IS HE OR SHE CONVENIENT? Is the prospect close enough to your office so that you can keep in touch conveniently and economically? Would the cost of providing service to the prospect be appropriate in terms of travel, entertainment, and unbillable time that would be part of the service? Would your convenience to him or her encourage the use of your service to produce a more profitable relationship? Your judgment on points like this can influence your decision to follow up on your first call or not.

Follow Up Interested Prospects

Your chances of success go up when you select prospects who have *demonstrated* an interest and keep in touch with them until *they* are ready to buy your service. Ask your prospect if he or she minds if you keep in touch from time to time. When you get a yes, your follow-up calls will take on some of the flavor of being responses to an invitation and your first step in building a sound relationship will have been taken.

Check with your prospect's secretary to find out the best times to call or visit. Your courtesy will be appreciated and you will be more likely to get a good reception during your follow-up efforts.

Establish the "tone" of your follow-up program by keeping in touch as a friend with another friend whom you like, respect, or admire. However, keep a professional and self-confident stance—you know your business and know that you know it.

Plan each follow-up call with the idea of strengthening the favorable impression you made during the first meeting. He or she won't buy your service until there is a definite need so any hint of pressure can work against you.

You can follow up with letters, telephone calls, and short social visits. You can keep in touch about once a month, and particularly when there have been changes in your prospect's organization that might mean that there is a need for your service. You may pick up some of those changes in the trade press or local newspapers.

The purpose of your follow-up program is to make your prospect remember you favorably when he or she is ready to buy. The decision to use your service is likely to be made in private when you are not there. So the idea is to leave your prospect each time with good memories about you and your service.

You can use different kinds of information to keep your prospect interested. A current case history from your work that is applicable to your prospect's situation or problems can build confidence in you. News items of interest with a brief note can jog his or her memory. News of your progress can build additional interest. A pertinent example of your work can help your prospect to remember you. A letter about what others with your prospect's problems are doing about them can help. Useful professional information that's organized and relevant can help.

When you make a short social visit, remind him or her of your previous visit and particularly any points made during that visit that got a strong and positive reaction. Your prospect will have been involved in lots of other activity between visits or calls from you and may not remember. The quality of the material you use to follow up reflects your interest in your prospect. That will be noticed and remembered.

You can also use short social visits to ask some questions, get your prospect to talk, and find out more about the current situation, interests, needs, and problems. The total impact of your follow-up program should emphasize your professionalism, interest in your prospect and his or her needs, and make it easy to call you in when the need arises.

It Can Boil Down to This

An effective selling program calls for a solid prospect list with clearly defined prospects; an organized approach to presenting your service; a practical way to open doors that suits you and your situation—a phone call that works, a sales letter that works, and referrals that work; a follow-up program that will help you get acceptance when your prospect is ready to buy. It is quite possible to test and automate many of these steps. Once you have them set up, you can keep selling with minimum use of your time.

A Cheerful Thought

Many professionals and specialists who are on their own have one major client, and that is all you need to start. Getting that client and knowing how to get more when *you* want to can give you the kind of peace of mind and sense of security that can keep you cheerful and build your income at the same time.

CHAPTER 6

Manage Your Service

There are specific management tools discussed in this chapter that can help you run your service by setting clear objectives, building specific plans, solving tough problems, making convincing decisions, and getting things done. There are also tools that can help you build your reputation by the way you deliver your service and make yourself valuable. And there are personal tools that aim at helping you to get satisfying results from reading, writing, observing, listening, remembering, and similar basic skills that can have a direct impact on the comfortable performance of your service. There are also some definitions of success to help you get started at writing your own. The brief highlights suggested here are for your immediate convenience and are intended as quick reminders. The same subjects are treated in depth in many excellent books that you may want to explore to further strengthen your management skills.

What Is Management?

Management is the identification and coordination of specific activities which will enable your service to run smoothly and reach the objectives you want to set for it.

Management of your service includes doing these jobs well: establishing clear objectives; developing practical plans for reaching those objectives; pricing your service to produce a fair profit; selling your service; testing the pricing, sales, and content of your service; delivering your service; controlling your time and costs.

The purpose is to make the *whole* work smoothly and efficiently. It is possible to make some of the parts nearly automatic and save a lot of your time. It is critical to keep the parts subservient to the whole.

Here are seven specific actions that can have a strong impact on how you are doing and how you are likely to do.

1. The careful expenditure of your time so that you don't put lopsided emphasis on what you like and do best at the expense of other necessary actions.

2. The development and testing of the content of your service and its adjustment to the specific needs of your personal marketplace.

3. The development and testing of your pricing so that your service produces a fair, reasonable, and continuing profit. This specifically includes attention to both your costs and your taxes, which are part of your cost of doing business.

4. The managing of expenses so that they don't get to a point where you are spending more than you are taking in.

5. Some time devoted to selling your service on a continuing basis. For instance, two calls a week on new prospects of 10 or 15 minutes each can add up to 100 calls a year and help to guarantee your security and growth.

6. Some time devoted to defining and then working toward long-term objectives. This need not take much time but it should be consistent and can be a real morale boost.

7. Some time devoted to providing and delivering your service to the best of your ability.

Your service is a business and it needs management like any other business. The alternative is like trying to dress in the dark when you can't quite remember where you put your clothes. It is important to strive for a reasonable balance. There is *no* limit to what you can be asked to do, but there *is* a limit to what you can do in a given day. Some time devoted to management of your service *as a whole* will help to guarantee that your service will prosper.

What Is an Objective?

An objective is a written definition that tells you where your service "as a whole" is going and when. It can also tell you what you want your service to be or become. An objective is specific and practical if you can financially afford to support the steps needed to reach it. Sound objectives demonstrate to you that your service is going somewhere, not just standing still.

You can have short-term objectives like the establishment of your sales program. When it is established it will not require too much day-to-day time. You can have clear financial objectives that give you something to shoot for. You can have performance objectives that help you improve the quality of your service. You can have long-term objectives that can help you focus your day-to-day work as you strive to reach them. Here is some room to jot down specific short-term objectives that can help you get started. If you put them in order of importance and work on them in that order, you can make things happen that will really help you to build quickly. Jot down your first two objectives here and get started.

Some Short-Term Objectives

_____

_____

_____

_____

_____

Build Specific Plans

An objective tells you _where_ your service is going; a plan tells you _how_ you are going to get there—the specific steps. A plan lets you put all your "ducks in a row" before you start so that you can see that you are not overlooking anything really important to results.

You can have short-term plans like the preparation of your selling program, which would consist of a list of jobs to be done in logical sequence: for instance, a clear definition of your prospects, the preparation of a solid and qualified prospect list, the preparation of sound sales materials such as letters or a small folder. Short-term plans like this tend to be highly specific and can be accomplished without the need to make too many changes. You can work out a timetable and jot it down on your calendar to help keep things moving.

You can have long-term plans like the establishment of sales and financial objectives for the first year. These long-term objectives tend to change because of events during the year. But it can help to have them as ideal goals so that you can focus your day-to-day efforts in their favor. Take a look at the first objective you wrote down and jot down your plans for reaching it in the room provided here so that you can start things moving.

Build Specific Plans

_____

_____

_____

_____

_____

Call In Outside Help

If you are like most of us, there are going to be *parts* of your program to develop your service that are not familiar ground for you. You can save a lot of time and trouble by calling in temporary consultants to help you with those parts only. For instance, an accountant can help you with pricing and setting up your books and relevant tax information. A marketing executive and effective writer can help you prepare sales materials. They can save you both time and frustration and help you move more quickly to the kind of results you want. When you bump into something that isn't familiar to you, hire a consultant to explain it to your satisfaction and, perhaps, do some work for you. Many will work with you on a time basis and their combined services need not be excessively expensive. On the contrary, if their services are satisfactory you may find that they are well worth it and economical in the long run.

How to Solve Tough Problems

This is an approach reserved for really tough and complicated problems. The fact is that developing information, defining problems, finding alternative solutions, making effective decisions, and learning to compromise are essential parts of a single and continuing process. Each step leads into the next. They all aim at finding workable solutions to tough problems.

It is important to see the logical sequence and relationships of the steps beforehand. Then you may feel more prepared to try to gain control of the *process* itself.

It also helps to recognize that the process has a beginning and an end. Here are nine steps aimed at solving a complex problem that you feel is important enough to deserve this kind of treatment.

WHAT IS YOUR IDEA OF THE PROBLEM? The direction you take at the very beginning depends on what you think the problem is at *that* time. With a really tough problem, it is especially important to write out your initial definition so that you can *see* it. It is also important to be willing to change that definition as you go along to make it increasingly clear, simple, and more accurate.

Try to avoid jumping to conclusions or exercising preconceived ideas or judgments. As much as is reasonable, try to avoid letting your own bias or desires distort your early definition of the problem or you will throw yourself off base at the beginning. Muster up as much objectivity about the problem as you can and move on from there.

DEFINE AVAILABLE FACTS. This means only those facts you have in hand that are clearly and obviously pertinent to the problem as you see it at this early point, facts that you feel are reasonably reliable. Make sure that you separate facts from your opinions or just plain wishful thinking. Write down the key facts so that you can *see* them. When they are safely on paper you may feel more relaxed about taking the next step without cluttering up your mind with the strain of trying to remember everything at once.

Look over the facts you have written down to see what is missing. What additional facts or information do you really need at this point? Where can you get them? During the development of these additional facts you may find that the problem has suddenly solved itself and disappeared. If it has *not* disappeared, you may find that the problem itself has become even clearer and that you are in a position to revise or update your first definition to make it even more accurate. You will also get a feeling that you are moving steadily ahead and gaining step-by-step control.

CUT THE PROBLEM DOWN TO SIZE. Some problems can be especially intimidating because of the way they are stated. Now, with the essential facts in hand, you may be able to break the problem down into workable *pieces.* Then you can work on those pieces and avoid being intimidated by "the whole thing."'

DEFINE THE REAL PROBLEM AND AN IDEAL SOLUTION. This step can help you define the problem again in the light of the information you have at *this* point. Bring it out in the open where you can see it more clearly. Use practical "what, where, when, why" viewpoints so that you can get a solidly balanced picture. With this information you may find yourself in a strong position to define an ideal solution. This ideal solution gives you something to aim for as you move ahead. It will give you a target or a sense of direction that can help build your morale as you work along.

DEVELOP SOME SOLUTIONS TO THE REAL PROBLEM. Keeping the total picture in mind, start to work out specific solutions. Here are some starting points to help you with this step. Define the elements of the problem as a whole and see if you can rearrange them to open the way to useful solutions. Make a particular point of trying to develop solutions based on facts. This can also be a good time to define the few additional facts you feel are needed. It pays to stay open to new evidence or information as you go along.

PUT YOUR SOLUTIONS IN ORDER. This means put them in the order that looks most promising to you at this point. This will help you decide which ones you want to work on first because they are most likely to produce the results you want. This is a real time saver.

TEST YOUR FAVORITE SOLUTIONS. Examine them from all sides. Take another look at the evidence that backs them up. It is important to keep your position regarding your favorite solutions free of wishful thinking. Try to be as objective as you can and avoid conclusions based on favoritism.

GET MORE EVIDENCE ON THE BEST SOLUTIONS. As you get closer to your final decision, take still another look at what backs it up. There may be a few additional facts or pieces of information you feel will help. Go out and get them but keep guarding against snap judgments and accept new evidence with an open mind.

MAKE YOUR SOLUTIONS VISIBLE. With a really complex problem and a variety of facts and information it is difficult to keep it all in mind. That's why it can help to make your best solutions and matching evidence visible. Then, you can *see* rather than just think about the choices just ahead.

Write each solution down on the top of a separate sheet of paper. Draw a line down the middle. Put the positive evidence on one side. Put the negative evidence on the other. Then, you can automatically see all your solutions and the evidence that supports each one.

Here's the advantage: When you can *see* all the solutions and evidence in one place at one time, you can get a quick and comprehensive view of each one. Then, you may find it easier to recognize the best choice. You may be surprised to find that sometimes you can have advantages that come from more than one solution.

Make Convincing Decisions

This means decisions that convince *you*. Try for optimistic decisions in the light of the evidence available. That's the best anyone can do.

Set a reasonable time limit that is relevant to the importance of the problem as you see it. Don't let it hang over you for long. Stick to your timetable and trust your judgment. Strive for a middle ground between acting too quickly and acting too slowly.

Try to recognize decisions that can be made on the basis of facts and logic only. You may be in a situation where facts and logic point with increasing obviousness to the right solution.

Most really important decisions are vague and call for judgments. For instance, the ultimate decision might rest on your feeling about the situation—your judgment based on previous experience. Just do the right thing as you see it at the time.

It may boil down to choosing between several practical and realistic solutions. It is here that compromise can help. Compromise means that you have to give up some good features of one solution in order to accept another with features that you like even better. So, compare the good features of each available solution and accept the idea that—whatever your decision—you are going to have to give up something you want. Make that compromise and move ahead.

Once you have reached a decision and want to take action it can help to suspend personal responsibility for the end result. Then you may feel free to put your energy into getting that result without a do-or-die pressure that can inhibit you.

Hold Good Meetings

Most professional and specialized services involve a variety of meetings for a variety of purposes. Here are some suggestions about running a meeting that will help you to make yours really work.

The idea of a meeting is to find sound solutions or conclusions that draw on the best knowledge and experience of everyone participating. Get to the point by making the subject, topic, or purpose of the meeting clear at the beginning. Tell everyone how long the meeting will be and stick to it. Make a point of encouraging everyone to participate actively. Ask quiet and encouraging questions to keep everyone on the subject. Questions can help to blunt domination by individuals. They also help bring out the knowledge and experience of participants who are shy—but who have particularly useful contributions to make. If things get hot call a five-minute break to cool everyone off. Try to keep discussion on a factual basis. This makes it harder for emotional types to maintain their position. When things sink to the opinion level arguments can easily break out and make your meeting hard to control.

Keep your meetings as informal as possible so that everyone will feel comfortable. If you are leading the meeting try to seat everyone where they can see you comfortably. Try to avoid a "special" place. Use first *or* last names consistently but don't mix them. It makes people uneasy. Near the end of your meeting announce a brief summary of agreements reached. Make these agreements or decisions quite clear because they are the results of your meeting.

As a final step, make clear who is going to handle any specific jobs that are the result of the meeting. Who is going to be responsible for the next steps? If another meeting is needed set the time and place before everyone disappears. Considering the subject and situation can help to keep your meetings as small and short as possible.

Get Things Done

Most of the secrets of getting things done are wrapped up in two words—common sense. For instance, you don't have to work too long and hard as long as you define and concentrate on a few really important jobs and get *them* done well. That's what produces results.

Define those important jobs in a list each day. Check that list to see that it contains items that will get results for you. This means the identification of specific jobs that will produce *visible results* for you each day. You may be surprised to find that a few items on your list will produce 90 percent of the results you really want. That's why working with a list pays off. It is the opposite of vaguely fumbling along.

Here are some general approaches that can help you evaluate your list. Start with the time available instead of the items on your list. Edit those items to focus on the really important ones. Capitalize on your strengths with the purpose of getting visible results. When items show up too often take a hard look to see if they are obsolete. If so, you can throw them out. Recognize that some items have their own special timing. Some jobs can only be done at the right time so schedule them when *they* are ready.

It is easy to overreact to a list of things to do and feel that you *must* get them all done. Try to avoid being compulsive about it and pace yourself carefully. Here are some thoughts that can help you keep your list interesting and enjoyable, despite pressure.

This is really a format for a list of things to do. You can probably save a lot of time and unnecessary work by giving your list some thought each morning.

The first items are the ones you *know* are important and will have a real impact on results. Maybe they involve deadlines, previous commitments, and the like.

Next come some personal items. Put aside some time for things you enjoy or have always wanted to do. One of those might be an ego builder where you rise and shine. Other possibilities are listening to music, learning a new sport or game, or doing some research to satisfy your curiosity. These are your rewards for getting difficult things done.

Next come your long-term objectives. Maybe you've been dreaming of some of them for quite a while. Put in some items that will help you make them come alive. This will give you a real sense of progress.

Don't forget the family. Maybe you should put in time to read to the kids, work on your hobby or start one, or pay more attention to your spouse.

When you have your list written down put it in order of importance as you see it in the morning. It will never hold up for the whole day but get off to a good start. You are almost bound to be interrupted at one point or another. Then just cross out the items you can't get done and move them up to the next day's list. Don't be surprised if they keep nagging you until you get them done. The purpose is simply to develop the *habit* of getting things done, which is one of the most essential qualities of success.

Deliver Your Service

Many professional and specialized services involve personal skills as well as solid chunks of egotism. This is what makes the delivery of service difficult and sometimes painful. When it comes to working on projects and assignments you can avoid tension and misunderstanding by quietly establishing some practical routines.

When you start an assignment get a clear definition of what that assignment consists of. Find out what you are to do very specifically. Write it down and get agreement. Don't hesitate to ask questions. Superficial people pose as if they know all the answers and then often endure all sorts of tensions wondering what to do later on. Avoid this position by getting a solid definition of the assignment at the beginning.

If you are working with a big organization ask your client to tell others about your assignment so that you will get both cooperation and recognition. This can save a lot of time and strain on you.

Report your progress when you are involved in difficult or complex projects. Getting your clients involved in the process of solving their problems helps to arouse their confidence in you and reassures them that you are doing the job well. Sharing some of the work-in-progress problems also stimulates them to develop some commitment to your solutions before you are through.

Treat everyone with courtesy and reap rewards of increased confidence. Make a point of building on this increased confidence in you by recognizing and protecting everyone's pride and dignity. Build confident relationships with all the people you meet on an assignment and avoid reliance on one person only, which weakens your position. The more people who know and like you in an organization, the stronger your position.

But, things sometimes don't work out. It is vital to develop tolerance and patience. So often the criticism of professional and specialized services is based exclusively on the subjectivity of the buyer. This is where self-control and patience can save the day for you. Remember, it is your client's money and like you he wants to spend it his way. If you accept that fact you can escape from a lot of bruising experiences.

Make Yourself Valuable

Deliver the finished results of your work when it is complete and in a form that your client can use immediately or as far along as agreed upon at the outset. This gives your service a reputation for reliability and helps make you valuable.

Focus your knowledge, experience, and service on what your client does well. Consider carefully whether your client will be able to make the most of your work by using his or her own experience. If your client is unfamiliar with your kind of service make certain to point out problems or trouble spots so that he or she can avoid them. This will help you earn his or her confidence and trust.

Every client is different and in a different situation. The more you know about your clients' problems the more easily you can co-ordinate your service with them. When you know clearly what your client wants to accomplish personally and professionally you can make your service even more valuable. It really comes from consciously thinking about your client and putting his or her interests and needs first.

When your client recognizes and becomes convinced that you are sincerely and genuinely interested in helping to achieve what he or she wants the whole atmosphere of the relationship will change. Many of the usual blocks and inhibitions drop away to make your service easier and more interesting to perform. You may be astonished at the hidden opportunities that appear. This will happen because you worked hard to earn a relationship of trust. This approach to making your service valuable can help you create long-term relationships that are equally valuable to both sides and give you a solid sense of security as well as continuing revenue.

Give Yourself Flexibility

Avoid painting yourself into a corner with exaggerated ideas about what you can accomplish. Pass up do-or-die situations which cause needless tension. If you develop an obsession to achieve certain results in a certain length of time you may face an emotion-draining battle that you can't win.

Being flexible under pressure is not easy. It means doing something different . . . consciously pacing yourself . . . seeking out a variety of sources of satisfaction. You are entitled to walk through a few obsessions (everyone does) but you are also entitled to come back with your dignity intact.

Study your special situation and schedule your work to avoid peaks and valleys as much as possible. Take a look at a particular assignment and give it the best you can in the time available and deliver the results with a clear conscience in order to avoid excessive frustration that can come from a drive for perfection.

Try to avoid putting demands on yourself that you cannot practically meet. For instance, seek other directions instead of insisting on one solution as the only acceptable one. If you feel that obsessive feeling coming up again stop and study it ... look at the causes and try to get some perspective.

If something isn't working, turn your attention to other jobs where you *can* get results. Get involved in them and then turn back to the difficulty with a fresh viewpoint and new energy. If this doesn't work, ask yourself why. Then seek out people you can trust, explain the situation, and see if they can help you. Ask them questions. Get a broader and more objective base of information.

In a losing battle, you can always beat a dignified tactical retreat. Seek achievements for the satisfactions they offer instead of the acclaim they might arouse. This attitude can help give you some flexibility when things get a bit sticky.

Produce Clear Writing

At one point or another you will probably need to write about your service. This can be difficult. It pays to develop a target and write to someone specific. This can make the act of writing easier because you will feel as though you are talking to a friend and then writing down what you would say instead of saying it. If you have a complicated service story imagine you are writing to someone who won't understand it at first. Then you will keep your words simple, which will make your writing more welcome.

Your writing will be easier to read and understand if you use words that stand for things people can see, feel, and touch, and that are familiar to them. Your objective is short, familiar words that tell precisely what you want to say. Don't be surprised if your first try doesn't work. Your writing will be easier to read if you keep your sentences short, about fifteen words. Remember, most people can read seven to ten words at a glance. That sentence was twelve words so you see how it works.

Almost every book on writing says this: Put action in your verbs and give color to your writing. Draw on your spoken vocabulary. Aim for simplicity and avoid long or technical words that reduce easy understanding and can look self-conscious. The purpose of writing is to get a message across, not confuse people.

When you visualize your reader give special attention to his or her experience with your subject. Then simplify your material accordingly. Take time when you want to write important material. Put it down on paper first. Then walk away and go back to it. You will then see new and better ways of doing it. Most writing takes a lot of rewriting to make its subject clear and simple.

When you have a finished product that you like, look even closer. Cut out unnecessary words. Take out any abstract words that make your writing vague. Eliminate unnecessarily technical words that your readers are not likely to understand. These steps will help you develop the obviousness and clarity that makes good writing easy to read.

Like everything else, writing takes time and experience. But it is one of your most useful tools when you want to get your service story across yourself.

Capitalize on Your Observations

Accurate observation can save you a tremendous amount of time and trouble. If you know what you want to accomplish and do a little advance research you will have a better idea of what to look for and can get even better results.

For instance, do you need information to solve a problem? Where will it fit in the development of an assignment or project? Will it help you develop information, ideas, or clear impressions that you need when you work on a project?

In the course of serving other people there are opportunities for time-saving observations of the people themselves, of working information, and of specific things that you are working with or on. It helps to get as many first-hand impressions as possible. Accurate observations can save you from making mistakes that waste your time later. When the subject is really important to you, your own observation is far better than second-hand reports or opinions.

When you see or hear something that is important and that you know you will use later, make a habit of repeating and reviewing it to drive it home in your memory. The objective is to make your observations stick in your memory so that you can use them when convenient.

When you want to remember useful information about people make note of what they say, the breadth and relevance of their knowledge and experience, their names and titles, their special interests and objectives. These are the kinds of observed and remembered impressions that can produce results when you do the work.

When you want to remember useful information from written material make note of why it is relevant and valid for your purposes. Check on the way it is organized. Look for themes, facts, and ideas that will give you the working information you need. While you are reading make note of where the material fits into what you want and are doing.

When you want to remember specific things or objects that are important to your work make note of everyday qualities like size, color, location, purpose, shape, or material—the kinds of qualities that can easily stick in your memory.

Get More out of Reading

When you are on your own, you sometimes need to get information from reading material. You can make that job more interesting if you remember what you want and recognize that reading is often the simplest and quickest way to your goal.

Many reading experts agree that one of the most effective ways to approach reading matter is to scan it first to make sure that it *does* contain what you want. You might ask yourself simple questions: Who wrote it? When? What were the author's qualifications? When you are satisfied on these points move ahead and take a look at the way the material is organized. If you are looking at a book, check the introduction, preface, and table of contents to get an advance review without strain on you.

When you are looking for usable information it is important to read with the deliberate intention of remembering what you read. This will help you recall the information later.

Examine the structure of the material. Recognize the themes, unifying ideas, and organization which will make the material more quickly coherent to you. Then the detailed information within the organization or structure will be easier to remember. If some parts are particularly important read them aloud to yourself. Then pause a moment and ask yourself what you have just read. This will help to impress the material you need on your memory.

Let Your Memory Work for You

A good memory can save you hours of extra work and sometimes a lot of nerve-wracking guesswork when you are trying to remember and respond to spoken requests from your client.

Your memory works much like a muscle: the more you use it the better it gets. Deciding that you want to improve your memory sets you off to a good start. On the practical side you may want more reasons. Will a good memory really save you extra work? Will it help you solve problems more conveniently? Will it help you get more done in less time? Will it enhance your reputation while making your day-to-day work more satisfying? If these and some of your own reasons are convincing to you that is all that counts.

A memory doesn't work in isolation. It comes from paying *close* attention to things you hear, observe, read, and study. They *all* contribute to the content of your memory. You can improve your memory by getting strong first-hand impressions. When you get brand-new information you want to remember, read it aloud. You will be driving the material home in your memory. It is simple but it works. Do it when the material or impression you want to remember is fresh and new.

Listen and Get Results

Quite logically, good listening is paying close attention to what you hear. It is also being interested in what you hear and responding to the speaker as an individual. Let him or her know that you want to hear and respond by showing that you are getting the message.

Don't you appreciate it when people let *you* know that they are getting your message? Your response can open up unexpectedly easy ways to get the information you need to work with. If you listen with the intention of remembering you may get even more useful information. This can be invaluable when you receive verbal instructions from a client or need to discuss critical problems connected with your work. When you listen with sympathy and understanding you are helping to relax the speaker and encouraging additional response.

Try to pay full attention without breaking in with your own ideas. If you listen thoughtfully *first* the speaker may well listen to you with more attention later. You may find that listening is just what you need to open up information and interest that would be beyond your reach otherwise. Besides, good listeners are much more welcome than big talkers.

Get Useful Answers

The art of asking questions can help you produce the information you need to do a job more quickly. Good questions get you to the heart of the matter to find out what your client really thinks. Be sure to make clear *why* you are asking questions so that your client will feel free to give you solid answers.

Before you start, think about your client's situation a bit. Pose your questions after your client has had his or her say and you may get a more attentive and responsive reception. Focus your questions on your client's strengths as you understand them and you may release oceans of useful information. Don't overlook the opportunities to respond so that he or she knows that you understand. Ask brief and encouraging questions to keep the conversation rolling. Here are a few: Can you tell me more about that? For instance? What happened? What do you have in mind? Can you expand on that? The purpose is to keep your client or prospect talking and comfortable at the same time. Questions are one of your most powerful tools in accomplishing this goal.

Make Your Voice Convincing

Your voice tells more about you than you may realize. It reflects your morale, your education, and the sincerity of your convictions.

A warm and friendly voice helps your listeners to relax by offering confidence and reassurance. When you talk slowly and clearly your listeners are more likely to understand you easily. That means that you are really communicating.

Your voice is one of the simplest and most direct ways to influence people. You can increase the effectiveness of your voice by developing a range. For example: Talk loudly. Talk softly. Whisper. Pause and offer dramatic chunks of silence now and then. This makes listening to you far more interesting.

When you look directly at people while you are talking, you make your words more convincing and you are more likely to be believed. When there is conviction and feeling in your voice people often react to it without showing it. Some people don't know how to react so don't expect too much.

Your voice can reduce tension by being quiet and friendly during an argument. A confident voice enables you to make a strong impression, creating trust that will help you build effective relationships.

Strengthen Your Notes

Taking accurate notes about complex problems and situations can save you hours of doubt and guesswork. Your notes may define an assignment, tell the results of a meeting, spell out what you are to do, or organize information for a presentation.

You may take your notes from conversation or from written information. The better you understand, the easier it is for you to complete your job. Here is a simple note-taking format that may save you some time. Just draw a line down the middle of a sheet of paper and put your own ideas on one side and the ideas you gather from the speaker or writer on the other.

What goes on your side? Put down any questions you may have at the beginning. They may be answered as you go along. But jotting them down clears your mind for the material ahead. As you go along you may be stimulated by what you read or hear. Put the resulting ideas down and keep going. Keep your ideas and questions separate from incoming material so you don't get mixed up.

What goes on the other side? This is for information and ideas from the speaker or writer you are noting. Penetrate that information and those ideas by recognizing their order, logic, facts, and sequence. This will make the whole more coherent and easier to recall later. Don't try to get everything down. Keep your notes brief by concentrating on recording useful ideas, interesting facts, unusual themes that you hear or read about. Use simple and standard devices to make your notes clear to you: abbreviations, capital letters, small letters or numbers, whatever makes your notes easier to use later on.

If the subject is very important to you, read the most critical parts of your notes out loud to help you remember them. If you do this three or four times you will probably not have to worry about remembering. The purpose is to get and keep the information so that you can use it conveniently when you need it to do your job.

Write Your Own Definition of Success

When you are on your own you *can* write your special definition of success and make it reachable for you in your special situation. Such as: Success on your own is knowing your job, doing it well, and getting along with people. You can find success in the idea of developing your service over a period of time and take satisfaction in each step that gives you growth. You can discover success in the satisfaction of using your knowledge and practical experience to build the quality of your service. You can uncover success in the steady development of your own faith and belief in your service. You can experience success in the satisfaction of doing your work your special way. You can recognize success when you get results in parts of your service that were unfamiliar to you at the beginning. You can earn success by moving one step at a time and making a point of understanding each step. You can experience success by overcoming temporary failure which will give you renewed confidence.

These are examples of the kind of success you can enjoy along the way—success that can be both reliable and habit forming. If you build steadily you will confirm your strengths, lift your ego, and build your confidence.

After you get successful results you can look back at them and get the encouragement to move ahead. You can learn a lot about success by studying your own victories. Why not start here and write down your own definition. Be practical so you can reach your goal soon.

Write Your Own Definition of Success

_____

_____

_____

_____

_____

A Cheerful Thought

Good management can make your service run smoothly and deliver the results people really want. This quality can attract the interest and acceptance of important people and open opportunities for you at increasingly higher levels.

CHAPTER 7

Make Your Service Profitable

This chapter aims at helping you to establish *four specific records* that can give you clear information and help you avoid having your service turn into a hobby without your realizing it. These records also aim at providing your accountant with information needed to help you get maximum tax savings.

Four Records You Should Keep

1. An overhead (rent, telephone, office supplies, etc.) log to help you keep track of overhead costs, petty cash expenditures, and out-of-pocket expenses.

2. A project-opening log where you can record each project, your estimate for each project, actual billing, and your profit from each project.

3. A portable time and expense record to make it easier and more convenient to keep track of time and expenses as you go along.

4. A project-in-progress log where you can record your time and project-related expenses as the basis for billing your clients.

To put it another way, this is an approach for everyone who hates to fiddle with records and knows that they should keep some records as a matter of self-interest and a sincere desire to avoid the feeling that they are financing everyone in sight with their tax dollars.

What Should Your Records Tell You?

Your records should give you a solid basis for decisions that can help you keep your service profitable. Here are some specifics:

1. Your overhead log should show you what you are really spending for overhead ... where, when, and how much. It shows your cash flow. You should be able to see this critical information in one place at one time. It will tell you when unruly leaks show up so that you can trim your sails a bit before things get out of hand.

2. Each project-opening record should contain a project number, client name, brief description, your original estimate, the actual billing when completed, and your income from each project after you have paid expenses. It should help you identify projects that are profitable for *you* so that you can head in *their* direction.

3. Your portable time and expense record should make it easy and convenient for you to jot down time and expense information as you go along. This avoids guesswork, which can be embarrassing when you are asked by a client to support bills for your time.

4. Your project-in-progress log should give you *one* place where you can record your time (for billing purposes) and any other project-related expenses for materials, outside services, out-of-pocket expenses, or any other project-related cost that is billable to your client. There should be a separate project log for each project to help you avoid getting mixed up when you want to bill your services.

Open a Bank Account

The first step is to open a bank account for your service *exclusively.* Put all business income and expense payments through this one account. This means both overhead and project-related expenses. Your use of this account for these purposes *automatically* establishes a record for tax purposes. Keep the bank deposit slips in a separate envelope because they are evidence of income for tax purposes. Mark the envelope "bank deposits for" and the year. Write the "income source" right on each bank deposit slip to make your income sources even clearer for tax purposes.

There is a combined checkbook and accounting system (it is called a peg-board or one-writer system) that lets you automatically record all payments *when you write a check.* Ask your accountant about it. Otherwise, a standard three-to-a-page checkbook from your bank will do the job along with a few standard accounting sheets from a stationery story (see later).

What Do Financial Words Mean?

When you want to understand your own records, it can help to have some definitions of financial words that apply. You might want to check these definitions with your accountant so that you will both be talking about the *same* thing and can make real progress.

WHAT IS ACCOUNTING? It is a system of keeping records of assets, liabilities, income, and expenses through the use of a journal (for recording daily transactions) and a ledger for defining assets, liabilities, income, and expenses at a given time. Journals are usually kept daily. Ledgers are usually kept monthly by your accountant. A ledger brings all your records together in one place at one time. There are five categories or types of account involved in accounting. Here are some definitions for your use.

1. Assets: What you own.
2. Liabilities: What you owe.
3. Equity: What your business is worth at a given time (the difference between what you own and what you owe).

Items 1 to 3 are the basis of a balance sheet.

4. Income: The total amount you produce from sales.
5. Expenses: What it costs you to generate your income, including your overhead and all project-related expenses. To put it another way, expenses are what you spend to get your income into your hands.

Items 4 and 5 are the basis of a profit and loss statement.

WHAT IS A BALANCE SHEET? It is a statement of financial position at a given time, such as at the end of the financial year. *At that moment* you own certain things and you owe certain things. The balance sheet shows your exact financial position as of the date and time you select.

WHAT IS A PROFIT AND LOSS STATEMENT? It is a statement that tells you what happened financially during a specific period of time. It could be a week, three months, or a year. It can be developed whenever you want it.

WHAT IS A TAX DIARY? It is a daily record of expenses. You can record small cash items (such as taxis, meals, tips, etc.) in a tax diary or on petty cash vouchers. You can keep a tax diary in your pocket or on a desk calendar. The IRS loves tax diaries. They read them for plot.

WHAT ARE OUT-OF-POCKET EXPENSES? They are overhead items you charge on your credit card or that are billed to you by suppliers. They are directly related to the overhead of your service. They could include a lunch or dinner with a prospect, supplies like writing pads or a pocket computer or file cabinet. These expenses are entirely legitimate and are tax deductible when they are recorded properly.

WHAT IS PETTY CASH? It is the cash fund from which you pay for small everyday expenses. They could be taxi fares, a few stamps, or similar incidentals that are related to the operation of your service. You can record them in your tax diary or on petty cash vouchers. They are also tax deductible when they are recorded properly.

Establish an Operating Budget

A budget is a forecast of your expenses for a specific period of time like three months, six months, or a year—whenever you decide.

You are supposed to "measure your costs" as you incur them against the budget you have set up. You should compare your expenses and your budget as you go along and try to stay reasonably on target.

Here are some items that you might want to put into your budget when you start out. You will want to adjust this suggestion to your own situation.

ITEM	AMOUNT
Rent	$ _____
Telephone service	$ _____
Telephone answering service	$ _____
Stationery and supplies	$ _____
Legal services	$ _____
Accounting service	$ _____
Travel	$ _____
Entertainment	$ _____
Miscellaneous	$ _____
_____	_____
_____	_____
_____	_____

The purpose of an operating budget is to get a clear picture, avoid surprises, and make sure that your costs don't overcome your income. A sound budget can help you keep your service profitable from the beginning.

What Does the IRS Want to Know?

The Internal Revenue Service takes a simple position: no records . . . no deductions. To be specific, if you don't claim a deduction, you won't *get* it; if you can't back it up, you won't *keep* it. Read that again! Without records you automatically pay a maximum tax. With records you may reduce that maximum tax substantially. The burden of proof is on you, not the IRS. This is where your accountant can really pay off for you. He or she can talk "taxation" when you need representation.

The IRS wants convincing evidence of income and expenses. You can prove your income with your bank deposit slips with income sources (your clients' company names) noted clearly on them. There is usually no problem with standard overhead items like rent, telephone, telephone answering service, and the like because they are easily provable. It is entertainment, travel, out-of-pocket expenses, petty cash, and miscellaneous expenses that may be questioned. It is here that bills and the cancelled checks that paid them provide convincing evidence. As long as you also have receipts marked "paid" for items you paid for in cash or by check and notations in a tax diary, you are likely to be covered.

This is what the IRS wants to know about your entertainment expenses.

1. The name of the place
2. The date
3. The business purpose
4. The names of the people you entertained
5. The titles of the people you entertained
6. The name of the company or companies that your guests work for

This may *look* a bit formidable when you see it in writing like this. It isn't that difficult in practice. For instance, there is provision for all this information on the back of most credit card receipts.

You can jot it down in your tax diary as you go along. A typical notation might say: Lunch 7/12. Valley Restaurant. Talked about new accounting system. J. Burns, President. P. Scott, Comptroller. Beechwood Manufacturing Company.

It is largely a question of getting into the habit of it. The habit is easy to *resist*, which can be expensive. It is also easy to *do*, which can both save you an accountant's time and give you valid tax deductions.

Set Up an Overhead Log

Once you leave the house in the morning practically everything you spend during the business day is likely to be tax deductible *if* it is a legitimate business expense but only *if* it is recorded properly. This is one of the values of establishing an overhead log.

WHAT IS OVERHEAD?

Here are some typical overhead items: rent; telephone service, telephone answering service; office supplies like stationery, file cabinets, writing pads, etc.; entertainment, which may well be lunches or dinners with prospects or clients; miscellaneous expense items, those that don't fit under any specific category—tips to building employees at Christmas, for instance; everything that is not charged directly to a project. Here's room to list your special overhead expense items, those that will be used regularly in your overhead log.

1. _____
2. _____
3. _____
4. _____
5. _____
6. _____
7. _____
8. _____
9. _____
10. _____

The information that goes *into* your overhead log comes from your checkbook, your tax diary or petty cash vouchers, your credit card receipts, and any other receipts or bills marked "paid" (not unpaid bills) for legitimate business expenses for anything from rent to telephone service to your working materials and office sup-

Overhead Log for January

Date	Overhead expense items	Ck #	Personal	Rent	Telephone	Tel. Ans. Service
1 4	Realty Company	801		21000		
1 7	Your Name (salary)	802	50000			
1 9	Telephone	803			9640	
1 12	Your Name (petty cash for Dec. entered in their natural categories (office supplies for stamps, etc., and misc.)	804				
1 14	To credit card company for entertainment in Dec.	806				
1 15	Tel. Ans. Service	807				30
1 21	Hatch Stationery (supplies)	808				
1 23	Typewriter Rental	809				

How it works

Enter each item chronologically as you pay your bills along with the check number. Then "post" or enter the specific amount in the column (1,2,3,), where it belongs

The purpose is to define the facts for yourself and for the IRS . . . and avoid having your overhead suddenly turn into undertow.

The sample entries of a few items "posted" show you how it works. You may have different categories or accounts on the top of the columns or need more columns.

This is a standard accounting page. They are available in pads in most stationery stores and you can get one that fits your needs.

Column notes (in the money columns):

Use this column for your salary only.

Use this column for rent only.

Use this column for telephone only.

Use this column for tel. ans. service only.

Repeat the column headings on page 2 of this log (if needed). Add up each column here and enter the column totals on line 40 and again on line 1 of the second page of your monthly overhead log . . . and keep going.

	5 Office supplies	6 Entertainment	7 Misc.	8 Direct Project Expenses	9 Total	10–12
						The headings are categories or accounts. They should define your most frequent overhead costs. Consult your accountant to make sure that they will be tax deductible.
1					21000	
2					50000	
3					9640	
4	2255		1418		3673	
8		11560			11560	
10					3000	
11	5860				5860	
12				3000	3000	

Use this column for office supplies and working materials only.

Use this column for entertainment only. Keep it as clear as a bell because the IRS is very interested.

Use this column for petty cash and small out-of-pocket expenses only. If a big item shows up, start a special column for it. Again, the IRS is interested.

Use this column for project related expenses so you have a record of payment when you have need for only a few project expenses.

Use the "total" column to balance things at the end of the month.

Enter each number in each column on its line in this column as well.

When you add up the total of each column separately they should match or balance with the total of this column.

plies. You record them only when you pay them. Then you record the name of the person or company you are paying (the payee), the check number, and the amount. You will see where and how in a moment.

How to Handle Petty Cash

This overhead log operates on a monthly basis, so you can accumulate petty cash entries in your tax diary or on petty cash vouchers on a monthly basis. If they are *not* recorded, you can't get a tax deduction for them. Collect them every month. Add them up. Put them in an envelope marked "Petty Cash For" and the month—if you are using petty cash vouchers. Write a check to yourself for the total amount and get this outlay back. At the same time (when you write the check) you will be establishing a record for IRS purposes.

How to Handle Out-of-Pocket Expenses

Petty cash and out-of-pocket expenses can mean the same thing. It can be confusing. Here they have been made deliberately different to make things clear. Here, out-of-pocket expenses focus on the supplier bills you incur for materials and supplies. Keep the supplier bills and credit card receipts together on a monthly basis. The checks that pay supplier and credit card bills are your evidence that backs them up as tax-deductible expenses. Set up another envelope clearly marked "Out-of-Pocket Expenses" and the month. This monthly accumulation of bills and credit card receipts with the checks that paid them is the evidence you need for IRS purposes.

Keep monthly envelopes for both Petty Cash and Out-of-Pocket Expenses with *their* monthly log. Then you will have both a convincing record and evidence of how the money was spent to help you stay on solid ground with the IRS.

Pay Yourself a Salary

Salary is also recorded in your overhead log. You write the check to yourself (not cash) and enter it under "personal" in the log. This establishes a record. Keep your home expenses away from this log. Make the log work exclusively for you and your service so that things don't get mixed up. Here is an example of a monthly overhead log with a few entries so that you can see more clearly how it works. You name the items first (who the checks are being paid to) and then enter the amounts under the appropriate columns when you pay them. It works on a chronological basis as you pay your bills. If you fill up one column on a page add up all the columns. Enter their totals at the bottom of the page and again at the top of the *next* page and keep going.

Start a Project-opening Record with Clout

This means one place where you can record the opening of new projects as they come in. It should show standard information like the date, project number, client, and a brief description of the project.

Then give it some clout. Add columns for: (1) your original estimate, (2) actual billing when the project is completed after all changes and adjustments but without sales taxes if they apply, (3) the dollar value of your time, (4) direct expenses you incurred in doing the work.

Project the profit to you after direct expenses are paid. This record can help you sharpen your estimates as you go along. It can also help you identify the kinds of projects that are most profitable for you to handle so that you can head in *their* direction. Here is an example to show you how this kind of project-opening record looks and works.

Start a Project Time and Expense Record

Here is a flexible format where you can jot down both your time and billable project expenses as you go along. Later, you can enter this information in appropriate job logs for future billing purposes. This chart is intended to be totally portable so that you can jot down your time and expense items before you forget them and know that your billing is solidly backed with current information. It helps you to avoid the pressure of guesswork, which can put you on the defensive when a client asks to see supporting background for your billing.

Set Up a Project-in-Progress Log

This is a running log of activities and expenses for each project. Make one log for each project so that you won't get mixed up when you have several projects going at once.

Project Opening Record

Date	Project #	Client	Description	Original Estimate	Actual Billing	Dollar Value of Your Time	Direct Expenses	Project Profit
5/16	843	PKT	20-page flip-over sales present-ation	$10,000 (Estimate for 20 printed copies)	$14,000 (Moved up to 100 copies with special cover)	$2,500 (For re-search, prep-aration and writing)	$10,000 (For design and print-ing)	$500 from your time. $1,500 from markups.

Portable Project Time and Expense Record

For week starting _____

Client	Project #	Date	Activity or billable item	Your time in hours or days							Billable Expenses
				M	T	W	Th	F	Sat	Sun	
Pkt	843	7/5	Meeting/outline		3						
ACB	840	7/6	Lunch/Music Sel			2					$27.50
P.C.	841	7/6	Meeting/New Proj			4					
T.R.	846	7/7	Outline for JR				3				
P.C.	841	7/7	Started D.M.				4				
J.C.	842	7/8	Speech/writing					6			

Keep this portable record daily to avoid guesswork. Once a week or as you see fit you can enter the content in appropriate project logs for billing purposes.

Establish a clear basis of operation. You can charge for time you are actually working on client-directed problems. Charge for your time during a working lunch. Charge one half of travel time to client offices if they are local. Operate the same way your client pays his, her employees. You may want to charge a little extra for weekend work or special rush assignments. This means a little more on your hourly rate. Make your method of operating clear to your client. Make it fair. You are likely to get acceptance.

This is the one place where you consolidate your billable working time doing research, consulting, solving, designing, planning—or whatever you do.

This is also the one place to record all expenses that are billable to your client. They could be payment for materials, special supplies, out-of-pocket expenses for travel or copies of material—they are whatever expenses you pay in the course of completing the project.

Keep all receipts for all expenses in a separate envelope (clearly marked with project number, client, and "billable expenses for Project #") and keep it with your project-in-progress log. The purpose is to have a place to put receipts instead of winding up with a shoebox full of "goodies" and have to spend hours sorting them out later.

Two different formats are given here for project-in-progress logs. Format 1 is intended for use when you do the work yourself and have few outside expenses. Format 2 is more extensive and intended for use when you have a major project and need outside suppliers and professional help.

FORMAT 1

Here is the first project-in-progress log format. The purpose is to show you what it looks like and how it works. *Activity* means your working time on the project. *Expense item* means a small outside expense for copies, taxi fare, and the like that are really billable to your client. Look at them carefully before you bill them. Sometimes small amounts like this should be part of your overhead and would be inappropriate to bill in the light of certain situations. But you should record them anyway because they are legitimate overhead expenses and tax deductible. Put them in your tax diary and run them through as part of your regular overhead. Then you can claim the tax deduction for them.

This first type of project log, for use when you do most of the work yourself with few billable expenses, is set up on a standard accounting page (available in pads in most stationery stores).

HOW TO HANDLE SALES TAXES. If sales taxes apply to your kind of project and you receive those taxes from your client, just "park" them in your savings account until it is time to pay the government—usually quarterly. If you let sales tax funds pile up in a checking account, you might accidentally spend them for something else and have a real problem when they come due. Indicate sales tax

Date	FORMAT 1 Activity or Expense Item	Time	Item
	A project-in-progress log for use when you do most of the work yourself with little or no outside expense. Establish a separate project log for each project so that you won't get mixed up when it comes to billing your service.	Use this column for your bill-able time only. Use 15 minute segments.	Use this column for expense items only.
5 17	First meeting to discuss project and define information sources	115	
5 18	Discussion with JSM, TRS and GW to get specific background	615	
5 23	Study of background material and prep-aration of experimental solutions	600	
5 24	Study and preparation of more solutions	630	
	Copies of 12 pages of material		475
5 29	Lunch discussion with GW to show material at Holiday Inn		2250
6 10	Meeting with GW/JSM and TRS to review solutions and select specific direction for further development	300	
6 18	Development of selected solution	200	
6 19	Development of selected solution	200	
6 23	Meeting with GW to review above	100	
7 1	Billed 28 hours @ $50 hr = $1,400. Decided not to bill copies and lunch - seems inappropriate. The entry below will be part of the next bill.		
7 5	Change of direction requested by company president. Development of new solutions to reflect content of this request.	615	When you get to the bottom of a column add both columns and put their totals on line 40 and again on line 1 of the next page and keep going.

payments to your savings account by entering them as an item: "Sales taxes, check number and amount" in the Item column. The purpose is to avoid worrying about accumulated sales taxes.

FORMAT 2

This second project-in-progress log format is used for complex projects where you hire outside professional help as well as outside suppliers of specialized services. Many such projects operate in natural steps and can be estimated accurately on the basis of those steps. They are often changes in the course of the work that affect both estimates and costs. Both of these "facts of life" are reflected in this format.

There is provision for estimating the steps. To get started, you can write in the estimates for your time, then for the outside professional help you use and other outside suppliers on line 1. You can do the same for subsequent steps when they come into focus and you are able to develop estimates for them. There is also provision for changes in direction as the work progresses. Just write in the date and highlights of the change. If it is unusually complicated, write yourself a brief dated memo (with a copy to your client) describing the change so that you won't forget what was done and when. There is also provision for sales taxes and a contingency (often about 20 percent or so) to add to your estimate so that everyone can avoid surprises.

Column 10, on the far right, will give you the totals of the different steps as you go along. You can use this column as the basis for your actual bill to your client. There is also provision for recording check numbers when you pay *suppliers to you* in the course of the project. In order to be specific, this example has been set up as a project for the preparation of a slide presentation needing outside design and various suppliers.

Who Is Audited by the Internal Revenue Service?

An audit is an examination of records. The purpose here is to provide information about how the IRS works so that you won't be surprised. Paying taxes is part of your cost of doing business.

There are probably about 190 million taxpayers in the United States. The IRS uses a computer to select taxpayers for an audit. This works much like "sampling" a market. A small number (compared to the total 190 million) are selected. The names are picked

objectively by a computer and the IRS does an audit on *those* selected names. The computer doesn't pick on anyone, it just picks
names.

The IRS also goes on dignified binges where it concentrates on
the returns of groups which are in a position to run up unusual expense claims. For instance, the IRS might audit doctors, lawyers,
and other identifiable groups. They might concentrate on certain
types of activity, certain industries, or professions where high income and expenses are frequent. This could mean sales operations,
restaurant organizations, and the like. The IRS regularly audits almost everyone with really high incomes.

The emphasis of IRS auditing activities changes from year to
year according to policies from within the IRS and what is happening that they feel deserves special attention. You will be audited if
the computer picks your name for an audit. It can also depend on
what the IRS sees in your return. Accountants and Internal Revenue Service professionals who are accustomed to looking at figures
and records all day long can "sense" when something is illogical or
inaccurate. They are experts at spotting things that are out of line
from just looking at the situation and the numbers.

Clear and straightforward records are your best bet in both the
short and long run. They can also give you some peace of mind in
case the initials IRS tend to make you a bit nervous.

Your accountant is also an expert and he or she is on your side.
A vital part of the job is reducing the taxes you have to pay.

Where to Get Tax Information

Try to avoid resistance to the IRS when it comes to getting information. It is the source of a lot of free information about starting a
business and particularly about how to handle entertainment and
miscellaneous business expenses. Don't hesitate to call the local office of the IRS for this material. You are likely to get a polite information officer who has nothing to do with auditing your taxes. Don't
be afraid that someone will pick on you later. The information is
available, free, and can be very useful when you start out.

What Happens If You Can't Pay Your Taxes?

Suppose tax payment time comes and you just don't have the funds
because an important client hasn't paid your bill yet. What really
happens? The IRS has thought about that! It doesn't come in and

				Outside profes-sional help	Outside Suppliers	2 + 3 Your o side c
Date	Activity or Expense Item	Ck #	Your name			
	Estimate: Step 1					
	Step 2		A project-in-progress log format			
	Step 3		when you use outside professiona			
	Step 4		help and suppliers.			
	Change dates:		Establish a separate project log			
	1. Note date and highlight		for each project so that you don			
	2. of change here. If it is		get mixed up when it comes to			
	complex, write yourself a		billing your project.			
	3. dated memo about it so you					
	4. won't forget and send a					
	5. copy to your client. If a					
	new estimate is needed					
	send that, too.					
	How it works		Use this	Use this	Use this	Use t
			column	column	column	colum
	Enter your first estimates on		for your	for esti-	for	to en
	line 1 for as much of the		billable	mates	estimates	and a
	project as you can estimate		time	and pay-	and pay-	up th
	at that time. Then, as your		only.	ment of	ment of	total
	project progresses, add			outside	outside	your
	additional estimates as they			profes-	suppliers	outsi
	become practical. Enter			sional	only.	costs
	estimates for outside profes-			help	This	
	sional help and suppliers on			only.	could be	
	line 1 and the next lines for				for	
	the next steps. This gives				materials,	
	you a clear and dated reference				services,	
	point.				produc-	
	Enter your own time for dif-				tion help.	
	ferent activities as you go					
	along. This will give you a					
	record for billing purposes.					
	Enter outside professional help					
	and suppliers bills as you pay					
	them.					
	Keep professional and supplier					
	bills in a separate envelope					
	with this log - they will help					
	back up your bill to your					
	client. Tell your client about					
	this record and say that it is					
	open for inspection at any time.					

FORMAT 2

our arkup	Out-of-pocket expenses & supplies	4+5+6 Your total costs	Sales Taxes	Contin-gency	Total	The headings at left should show your major out-side costs. Consult an accountant to see that you have it right and will get maximum tax savings.
e this lumn to d your rkup out-de ofes-onal lp and ppliers. is is ur pay-nt for king spon-bility r their rk.	Use this column for project-related out-of-pocket expenses and any special materials needed to do the job.	Use this to enter and add up columns 4,5, and 6 to get a clear total of all your outside costs.	Use this column for sales taxes that apply. Ask your account-ant. Put these amounts in your savings account immedia-tely and get int-erest until they are due.	Use this column to add 20% or so to your estimates so that you and your client can avoid surprises.	Use this column to get the total of all other columns and as the basis for your bill.	

1
2
3
4
5
6
7
8
9
10
11
12
13
14
15
16
17
18
19
20
21
22
23
24
25
26
27
28
29
30
31
32
33
34
35
36
37
38
39
40

pick up your desk and chair or it would have used furniture all over the state of Arizona and then some. There are standard procedures. The IRS can assess you interest on the taxes you owe. It can also assess penalties but that depends on the situation. Your accountant can tell you about these procedures and it can help to understand them clearly so that you are not surprised. Knowing the facts is far better than being worried about them.

Luckily . . . There Is Help

After looking this chapter over you may feel that you want help. You are absolutely right. It is very difficult for most of us (except accountants) to seriously start a professional or specialized service without help from an accountant.

To help you avoid surprises, here are some questions an accountant might ask you:

1. What are you going to do?
2. What kinds of clients are you seeking and what will you do for them?
3. What is the basis of your billing?
4. Will you use outside help? Who? When? What will they be doing?
5. What kind of materials or supplies will you have to buy to perform your service?
6. What types of expenses do you expect?
7. How often do you need financial information?
8. What are your record-keeping capabilities? Good? Bad? Don't ask!

This is just a start, but it will give you some idea so that you can prepare as you see fit.

An accountant can define local, state, and federal taxes that apply to your service. He or she can tell you whether you need any special licenses or registrations with government agencies. He or she can show you how your social security taxes will be paid when you are on your own. He or she can help you set up your records for maximum profit with minimum tax bite. He or she can answer your questions about what you have read here. You are wise to draw in an accountant very early in your planning.

A Cheerful Thought

The time you spend establishing and understanding your records and then learning to keep them up to date in minimum time will pay off handsomely. The cheerful thought: This understanding can give you genuine control of your service and help you identify *reliable* sources of income. It has been done by others. You can do it too.

CHAPTER 8

Build Your Own Morale

There are suggestions in this chapter that aim at helping you to cope with worry, tension, criticism, and disappointment when you are on your own. These suggestions are followed by others which aim at helping you to encourage yourself, build confidence and enthusiasm. Then, there is a cheerful thought to take along with you on the way to success.

Why Is Going on Your Own Scary?

Here is an assortment of reasons which reflect that fact that everyone responds differently to the situation of going it alone.

The truth is that many professionals and specialists who know their fields never have the time to learn some of the skills they need to go on their own. Learning new things can cause concern. Then, there's the change itself. That change may include a move from a job where there is recognition, personal and economic support, and familiar routines. When the reassurance of familiar routines is missing there can be short-term worry and anxiety until they are *replaced*.

One of the primary purposes of this book is to help you overcome the touchy parts by establishing new routines and developing new skills and other specific actions which can quickly *replace* the natural concerns that often surround the first steps.

What Is Morale?

Morale is a feeling of confidence that *you* can do it. Good morale can be the spark that lets you attract optimistic and constructive people to your side and really enjoy performing your service. You can be confident about things that you do well one at a time. There is no reason why you can't be confident about new tasks by learning about them first and then *doing* them so that you really understand them to a point where you are comfortable and confident. Then you will have reason to believe that your morale will move up accordingly.

Turn Away Worry

What is worry? It is a feeling that something isn't under control. Worry isn't the same as thinking a problem through to bring that "something" into control and make worry diminish.

A worrier is basically a pessimist. Worriers look at the bad side of things. Optimists look at the good side of things. Both can be equally unrealistic. A basic approach: split it down the middle and put in a little reasonableness and logic. Here are six ways to cut down on worry.

1. Get the facts straight. Generalities unsupported by facts can cause a lot of worry. You can do something about that by getting the concrete evidence that will give you a realistic picture.

2. Get the words clear. Needless worry can come about simply through misunderstanding what other people really said or meant. It can be helpful to ask them to repeat things until you get it clear. Words mean different things to different people. You can do something about that.

3. Find workable solutions. Actively looking for good solutions to what is worrying you can cause worry to diminish ... just because you know you are *doing something* about it. When you do things that are within your control, worry tends to be displaced. If you are trying to do something that is impossible, you may be able to identify it as such and avoid keeping your worries alive forever.

4. Make your choice. Make a clear-cut decision. The fact and act of that decision may cause a particular worry to disappear. Yet, some worries may be truly beyond your control. When this is really true and you recognize and accept it, your worry may diminish. You may have to accept the fact that there is nothing you can do about a particular worry and let it go its way.

5. Don't worry unduly about what other people say. Try to control your worry on this point by recognizing the fact that you can never fully control what other people say. Sometimes they can't either. Maybe it's fair all around.

6. Don't worry about what other people do. Again, this is something that you can't control. If you accept this as a fact, worries on this score might diminish. The purpose here is simply to offer you some choices so that you can do something about worry when you start out on your own.

Tangle with Tension

What is tension? Tension is really too much of a good thing. That good thing is stress. Stress is something that comes from the outside and you can explain its source because it is really there. For instance, a close deadline on an important assignment can cause tension.

This is in contrast with *anxiety,* which comes from the inside. You cannot explain its source because it is *not* really there. It is imaginary but seems real.

Recognize that there are occasions when stress can be a good thing. For instance, it can help you develop a fast and invigorating work pace, rise to the occasion, develop the drive needed to get things done.

Here are some things you can do when tension hits.

Breathe slowly and exhale gradually while relaxing in a comfortable chair. This can help if tension is making you physically taut.

Do the exact opposite of what is making you tense. If tension is coming from too much work, concentration, too many problems and meetings, find something else to occupy you.

Do something mindless. The idea is to have something that engages *some* of your attention while you let your mind wander—a brisk walk, knitting, an amusing movie, hitting a few golf or tennis balls.

Tell someone who is sympathetic. Sheer verbalizing can tend to diminish or reduce the impact or internal pressure of it all. The act of having your say and sharing it can keep tension from just rolling around in your mind and help you get rid of it.

Listen sympathetically to someone else's problems. When you

lend a helping hand you will find that *your own tension* will tend to diminish. If you can help others over their troubles, you can believe that you can help yourself over yours.

Let hard work and vigorous exercise drain off anger and tension. Exercise where you really work up a sweat is a way of changing the subject away from the cause of your tension.

Do something that builds your ego. This is another way of changing the subject. You may find it in a community activity where your talents shine or participation in a church program or work on your favorite hobby—any activity that builds your self-esteem and that you enjoy.

Deal with Anxiety

As was said, tension is the result of stress and comes from the outside. It is based on real and provable facts, whereas anxiety comes from the inside. It is a feeling of fear without anything specific to be afraid of. The worst thing about anxiety is that it is treacherous. It can deceive some, for instance, by temporarily convincing them that they can't tackle a task that they've done successfully many times before. Here are some ways to deal with anxiety of a moderate degree. *Extreme anxiety calls for professional help.*

Share your feelings. Talk over the substance of your anxiety with someone who is sympathetic. Talking it out lets you "hear it" and helps to release some of the pressure on you. The fact is that anxiety thrives on silence, where it can escalate out of all proportion.

Listen to yourself. What *are* you telling yourself about the subject of your anxiety? Sometimes you can see that your own arguments are lopsided. You may see how unfair you are being to yourself. You may see how absurd or exaggerated your arguments really are. You may see that you are posing yourself an empty threat. You may see that some of your arguments are valid, some pessimistic, and some optimistic.

Write it out. Sometimes you can get relief by writing out the substance of your arguments about your anxiety. Then look them over. Where are they true? Where are they obviously emotional? Challenge your arguments. What *are* the facts? What *can* you do about them that is within your control? What *is* an ideal solution? What *is* beyond your powers? If you don't have a solution and know that you can't get one, you can accept that fact and move on from there. It can help to turn to something else where you can produce satisfying results. Go to church or some other calm surrounding. Come to a decision that can help you put that anxiety behind you.

Stop fiddling with it. Turn to something else and let the substance of your anxiety simmer on its own. Put it away. Put it to rest. You can be sure that doing something else can help because the substance of your anxiety will look different when you return to it.

Grapple with Disappointment and Failure

What is disappointment? It is expecting something important that you really want and not getting it. Sometimes, it is the result of expecting too much in the first place. You are entitled to blow your stack a bit to clear the air. But watch your timing. Don't let a particular chunk of disappointment keep grinding on you. Set a time limit and go on to the next things to do. Ask yourself a few private questions. Did you have the right to expect what you wanted? Was there too much wishful thinking? Did you really work hard enough to get it? Were you justified in expecting it in the light of the choices open to the *other* side?

Take a look at the other side. Try particularly hard to see at least some of their probable opinions. How did it look to them? How did they react? Why? What did they do? Put yourself in their shoes.

Admit mistakes. Disappointment can sometimes point up a mistake, weakness, or misjudgment on your part. Admit it quickly and then repair it quickly. The penalty is to go on the defensive. You can't justify it and you know it. If you could justify it, you would be able to go on the offensive. Admit it and move on.

Avoid self-pity. Disappointment dents your ego and tampers with your self-respect. You are entitled to "mourn" a bit. But keep a firm grip on your timing. Never let it go for more than a week, if that.

What is failure? Failure is a form of disappointment. You didn't get what you really wanted. To put it into some perspective: Why don't you feel a sense of failure when you don't get something you don't care much about? Failure occurs only when it really matters to you. Failure can also occur when you weren't able to deliver what you said you could. The best defense against this kind of failure is the knowledge that you did everything you could and that the results occurred for reasons beyond your control. To make this defense work you have to be on really solid, factual ground.

Disappointment and failure are subjective to some extent. Have you ever noticed how someone else's failure looks to you? Your own disappointment or failure *never* looks as severe to an outsider as it looks to you from the inside. The idea is to "join the outsider" and take a look from there. It's a good way to draw the sting, cut or diminish disappointment.

Coping with disappointment pays handsome dividends. It strengthens your belief in yourself and your self-respect. It reduces your worry about the idea of failure. It teaches you new things about yourself and your work that you can use soon again. Accept. Forget. Move forward. This is probably the most practical attitude you can adopt toward either disappointment or failure.

Cope with Your Critics

What is criticism? It is supposed to consist entirely of constructive ideas and suggestions from the knowledge and practical experience of qualified people. It is supposed to start with what is good and move from there to point out areas that need strengthening. Such critical comments aim at determining the best course of action. A lot of people are conditioned by their own experience to think that criticism *must* be negative. In fact, some people are convinced only by negative criticism.

Qualified criticism can produce new ideas and new ways of doing things. It can steer you away from trouble. It can add to and strengthen existing plans, programs, and ideas. It can hurt, too. It can cut through personal blind spots to reveal something that can be extremely valuable.

The truth is that most people overlook 90 percent of what is good in a proposition to concentrate on the 10 percent that may be bad. It's lopsided. What can you do about such incoming criticism? Here are four kinds of critics and some ways to look at them.

THE CONSTANT CRITIC. Some people have the *habit* of criticizing. They are often pessimists and it is *their* problem—not yours. It pays to avoid taking such critics too seriously. It is their habit talking. They accept you despite their constant criticism.

THE EMOTIONAL CRITIC. This kind of critic often resorts to stinging comments and hurtful words. It is difficult to stay calm in such a situation. But try to make a point of *never* responding emotionally when this occurs. Don't deny someone else a probably much needed emotional jag. But don't match it at the same time. Instead, be as calm and logical as possible. Find *something* to agree with—a part of the criticism that you feel is valid. This tends to upstage your critic.

THE MEAN CRITIC. Envious and destructive people will sometimes try to build themselves up by criticizing you. Try to cancel their game at the start. Again, find something to agree with and disarm the critic. You may be dealing with an SOB, but he may have an excellent point.

THE QUALIFIED CRITIC. When the critic has something to say of real substance that is obviously aimed at helping, listen carefully . . . learn as much as you can . . . ask questions . . . give the criticism a warm reception. Express your appreciation afterward.

Can Tolerance Help You?

What is tolerance? It is the ability to accept the standards others have found satisfactory, useful, and workable for themselves—just as you have found standards that you feel are workable for you. Tolerance is mutual acceptance without judging or prejudice.

Tolerance is your ability to accept other people's ideas, habits, actions, reactions, or conclusions on important matters without judging or necessarily agreeing with them. This means ideas, actions, and habits on the positive side as compared to negative ones that could cause injury.

This kind of tolerance makes it possible to accept other people, work with them comfortably, and encourage them. Your acceptance of them increases their confidence in themselves and their acceptance of you.

Tolerance recognizes that others are different rather than difficult. It recognizes that each has different knowledge, experience, and ideas and has drawn different conclusions.

If you accept their differences, they are more likely to accept yours. The cultivation of this kind of tolerance lets you work with increasing calm and serenity and earn the cooperation and active help of more and more reasonable people.

It can also help you recognize and avoid disturbing overreactions and recognize situations that might not turn out to be practical or workable for you.

Tolerance attracts the interest and support of people who can make your work satisfying and successful. It can have a direct and continuing impact on your morale.

Give Yourself Encouragement

Get in the habit of encouraging yourself. This one habit can have a profound impact on your performance and the results you can get, as well as on your basic morale.

Why be so critical? The truth is that some people are far harder on themselves than on others. This is for *their* special consideration. It is also a fact that those who are less secure are often more severe in their self-criticism. It is a habit that can be broken. It takes perseverance, attention, and time.

The habit of self-criticism can come about naturally. You may have noticed that most people are quick to criticize others. In a way, criticism is more interesting than praise. It's lopsided. Most people get more criticism than praise. That's lopsided, too.

As a result, some people focus more on their shortcomings and not enough on their strengths. It's a habit. The challenge is to find a reasonable middle ground for yourself. One of the satisfactions of success is simply that it offers convincing evidence that you are on the right track. This evidence weakens the severity of self-criticism. The idea is to blunt excessive self-criticism first. Then turn more and more toward a balanced recognition of your strengths. Decide to stop judging yourself for good or ill and make a firm decision to keep encouraging yourself. This can create a new situation where you can comfortably look for your strengths.

For example, listen for signs that you are putting yourself down or putting unfair emphasis on your shortcomings and steadily bring things into a balance that is fair to you.

Learn to pat yourself on the back. Here are some ways. They may take a little getting used to. For example, make a point of stopping to enjoy the feeling of satisfaction that comes from a job well done. That satisfaction is encouraging.

Keep your objectives practical and within reasonable reach. Then work toward them by meeting your own expectations. This will give you victories that you can stop and enjoy along the way.

Deliberately look for things that will make you feel good about yourself and your work. They will tell you that you are really going places.

When you take responsibility for a specific decision and work to get results you will experience an encouraging sense of freedom. Take encouragement from that freedom and work to bring excessive self-criticism into increasingly firm control.

Build Your Confidence

What is confidence? It is a feeling that *you* can do something specific that comes from a combination of knowledge and experience that proves (to you) that you can do it. It helps to recognize that nobody is confident about everything they do despite some loud talk to the contrary. You can be confident about things you know and have experienced one at a time and build on that.

One of the results of genuine confidence is a feeling that you can make mistakes and accept temporary failure. You can accept them and treat them as temporary way stations on the route to what you want. Then you can examine them and learn from them with the safety and encouragement that come from the knowledge that you won't have to make those mistakes again. Get something out of your mistakes so they won't hurt your confidence or become exaggerated disasters.

In fact, genuine confidence comes from using mistakes to strengthen your understanding. Genuinely confident people feel free to ask questions and seek advice. They have frank exchanges with peers where they know that their knowledge and experience are intact, so they can look at the exchange as a learning experience.

Genuine confidence also comes from enjoying your share of success in what you are doing. This success, along the way, builds up to give you convincing evidence that you know what you are doing and acts as a breeding ground of still more confidence. Genuine confidence cannot be built easily, which is precisely why it cannot be destroyed easily either. Such confidence is a source of continuing strength that can meet mistakes and success. It takes work and maintenance to develop such confidence but then it becomes yours for keeps. Your own confidence is often instantly recognized by others and can substantially encourage their acceptance of you and your service.

Give Yourself Balance

Your attitudes have a lot to do with your morale and the development of a practical and comfortable sense of balance that can help you move your service steadily ahead. Here are some steps that aim at helping you develop useful balance. Look them over and see what appeals to you.

Concentrate on the development of practical objectives that are reachable in the light of your knowledge, practical experience, and resources. This can save you a lot of unnecessary frustration from too big a "gap" between what you want and what you can reasonably expect to accomplish on your own.

Work on the development of your *service* and what you can accomplish through *it* in the future. This can help you avoid difficulties that arise from too much concentration on yourself, the past, and, particularly, past mistakes. Going on your own lets you start a brand-new chapter.

Establish a habit of expecting the best because this is one of the simplest and most practical ways to earn freedom from self-doubt.

Get seriously interested in serving your clients to the *very best* of your ability for the opportunities that your sincere interest in them can create for both of you. Make a point of recognizing the strengths and weaknesses in your service and make steady improvements.

Accept your successes so that you can give yourself honest credit when you have earned it and build faith and belief in yourself and your service.

Build Your Enthusiasm

One of the chief values of genuine enthusiasm is the fact that it can *replace* nagging worries, anxieties, and other personal hobgoblins that haunt most of us. Those hobgoblins can capture too much attention and act as a brake on what you want to accomplish. That's why genuine enthusiasm deserves your attention. In fact, it can make a decisive contribution to your ability to perform and deliver your service.

What is enthusiasm? It is a feeling of satisfaction and confidence that comes from your work. It is the personal satisfaction that you enjoy from being "caught up" in work that *you* think is fascinating and worthwhile. It is seeing special personal possibilities and your kind of future in the work you are doing. It is a way to attract other enthusiastic and confident people. It is a way to encourage associates.

This helps to underline again the importance of basing your service on what you like and do best so that you have natural reasons for being enthusiastic.

Where does enthusiasm come from? Enthusiasm that really lasts can come from a variety of sources. It is there all the time and the idea is to take some actions that can encourage it to appear. Here are some from which to pick out a few that appeal to you, or develop your own ideas.

Sources of Enthusiasm

1. The use of your knowledge and practical experience to accomplish a purpose that you believe in can stimulate enthusiasm.

2. Doing your best to grapple realistically with a problem instead of just worrying about it can spark enthusiasm.

3. The increased confidence you get when you use your talent and ability to your *private* satisfaction can arouse enthusiasm.

4. Doing the necessary work to define practical and reachable short- and long-term objectives so that you can focus some of your day-to-day work on them will stimulate enthusiasm.

5. Working to make your objectives clearer and then getting relevant and visible results can create a large chunk of enthusiasm.

6. Planning that obviously saves your time and helps you identify and get important things done on time can produce a bank of convincing evidence that is a basis for enthusiasm.

7. Doing the drudgery that will help you find what you like and do best and using it as the basis of your service can give you a surge of enthusiasm. Don't be surprised to find a little excitement along the way.

8. Doing a job wholeheartedly can generate the kind of enthusiasm and momentum that makes it easier to tackle the next one.

9. Concentrate on your immediate tasks and make them more important than your other commitments. This can give your work the kind of dignity and prestige it deserves. This will open up the kind of freedom and perspective in which enthusiasm can grow naturally.

10. Don't let mistakes dampen your spirits. Use them to test, sharpen, and build your performance, giving you a solid reason for enthusiasm.

11. Failure is always temporary, as you know from your own experience. Use it as a means of recognizing mistakes with the knowledge that you won't have to repeat them. This will open the way to enthusiasm.

12. Success is always temporary, as you know from your own experience. Use it as a means of confirming your strengths which will offer you a sound reason for enthusiasm.

13. Put success and failure into perspective so that you know that you can continue to enjoy enthusiasm or not miss out for long.

14. Recognize that it is people who believe in you, trust you, and want you to succeed who will help you make real progress. That's why your genuine and unselfish interest in service to them and others offers a natural source in which enthusiasm can flourish.

15. Make a point of being the first to express belief and enthusiasm when you can do it sincerely. This creates an atmosphere in which other people will feel free to respond. Some people hesitate and can't be first because they have trouble expressing themselves. Don't be disappointed. It is their problem. You can start things moving by taking the first step yourself.

16. Taking the first step encourages other people to be enthusiastic and confident. They will appreciate it and you will enjoy working in a climate that helps get exciting results for everyone.

17. Determine to make doing new things an interesting adventure. This will give you the freedom to grow that will stimulate enthusiasm. There is a lot of satisfaction waiting for you when you try new things and succeed.

18. Tear down personal roadblocks and resistance in the way of your performance. Give yourself the freedom and advantages of flexibility that can meet new situations calmly and confidently.

Take a Shot at Maturity

When you are on your own, maturity can help you through those interesting times when you are learning new things. Maturity is an idea that can only be sought after. It reflects the steady development of attitudes that encourage flexibility, the acceptance of things as they happen. It fosters a realism that helps you to be unsurprised by events.

Having some ideas to work with can help when you are ready for them. Otherwise, they remain words in a book waiting to help. Here are some examples.

Try to accept individuals without being prejudiced beforehand or trying to judge them afterward. If you get too involved with yourself you may be paying only superficial attention to others and this can work against you.

Determine to build yourself and your service naturally instead of trying to copy someone else. Copying someone never works and can both appear unnatural and feel uncomfortable.

Make a strong determination to sweat out difficult problems

and projects as they come along. Put in a little faith and patience when you face discouraging setbacks and criticism.

Be quick to admit mistakes to yourself and others so that after the twinge you know that you won't have to be on the defensive.

Work on building a reputation for dependability so that your word is respected and you can build solid relationships that may open up unexpected new opportunities for you.

Try to avoid getting too involved in your service to the exclusion of other interests and sources of satisfaction. You may need them to help you develop flexibility if the going gets rough.

Work steadily on the quality of your decisions and stick to those that demonstrate that they are working.

Concentrate on developing your talent and skills to make yourself increasingly self-sufficient in the performance of your service. This will give you increasing independence.

Work steadily to develop a realistic idea of the value of your talents and ability and enjoy the kind of self-respect that will give you increasing freedom of action.

Set your objectives and define achievements on the basis of the satisfaction and personal growth they can offer you. Working to get the recognition of others can't compare with working to get results that satisfy you.

Develop patience and tolerance that will enable you to settle differences without anger and work with people in an atmosphere free of tension.

A Cheerful Thought

This book is an invitation to go on your own and succeed. It is an invitation backed by the knowledge and practical experience of bankers, lawyers, sales executives, top management executives, partners, professors, owners of services, and others. They are joined by this author in this cheerful thought: Now it is *your* turn to rise and shine.

INDEX

ABOUT THE AUTHOR

After twenty years of a successful career as an advertising writer, Richard Creedy set out to fulfill a dream he had had since graduating from high school: setting up his own business and being his own boss. Various attempts finally led him to work out the formula for setting up a specialized service to make best use of personal skills. He heads a consulting firm in New York's competitive business community.